Obama: First African American President

Successful Timing

SHEHU BANKOLE-HAMEED

iUniverse, Inc.
New York   Bloomington

iUniverse books may be ordered through booksellers or by contacting:

iUniverse
1663 Liberty Drive
Bloomington, IN 47403
www.iuniverse.com
1-800-Authors (1-800-288-4677)

Because of the dynamic nature of the Internet, any Web addresses or links contained in this book may have changed since publication and may no longer be valid. The views expressed in this work are solely those of the author and do not necessarily reflect the views of the publisher, and the publisher hereby disclaims any responsibility for them.

ISBN: 978-1-4401-6729-4 (sc)
ISBN: 978-1-4401-6731-7 (hc)
ISBN: 978-1-4401-6730-0 (ebook)

Printed in the United States of America

iUniverse rev. date: 11/18/2009

Preface

I am an African American who emigrated from Nigeria in 1998, when President Bill Clinton was still in office. The US economy was vibrant; jobs were plentiful all over the land. Like many of my community (African American) members, I changed jobs a few times (many after being laid off) and also learned new skills as a business analyst in IT applications.

A couple of years later George Bush was elected President. The economy went sour, first it was the recession, and next US went to fight a senseless war in Iraq. Soon, many middle class Americans began to feel the pain of economic mismanagement, just as many in Wall Street took bonuses before and after they set the Wall ablaze. There was real fear in the land; many Muslims felt trapped, and immigrants who thought that the US was their only safe haven started to doubt.

While these happenings gripped the land, some politicians again offered their services to Americans to save the nation. But only one candidate truly stepped up to the plate. He offered hope instead of fear; he preached calm rather than panic, and stressed unity in place of separation. We of the African community were quick to recognize these qualities in President Barack Obama, for many of us have lived through lying despots as politicians. We wanted to have an opportunity to say never again – or can we? Yes we can.

This book is an account of how I experienced the entire election process from the Primaries, through the Party Conventions to the General Elections. I wrote this book to capture my thoughts in my language Yoruba, but translated in English.

It may therefore contain some colloquial language. My sincere gratitude to all whose effort made it possible to write this book. I have attempted to discuss the contributions of unsung heroin Oprah Winfrey and that of African Americans to the election of President Barack Obama. I have analyzed in summary, the complex relationships between the candidates and majority of us in the African American community (those of us immigrants from Africa).

There are seven chapters in the book, the seventh chapter has been written to present the issues as current as they can be. I prefer to let the readers enjoy these issues as if they were still fresh.

My sincere gratitude goes to my wife Abiola, my children Olasubomi, Wonuola, and Agboola.

My dear, your contributions and that of our both parents, other family members and friends are noteworthy. Above all, I thank the Almighty Lord for his guidance.

Chapter 1

President Barack Obama.

The US Presidential elections of 2008 produced a result of monumental proportions. It sent a definite message of change, hope and inspiration. The voters chose Barack Obama as the 44th President of the United States of America and the first African-American to occupy arguably the most powerful office on the planet. Senator Joe Biden was tapped by Barack Obama to be Vice Presidential nominee of the Democratic Party, after he dropped out early in the primaries. He is a Roman Catholic, the first Roman Catholic Vice-President and the 47th US Vice-President.[1]

By the largest number of total votes cast ever, 64 million plus with over 53% of the votes, he won the hearts of millions of Americans[2]. Without doubt President Barack Obama won the election with overwhelming majority of the states, 28 in total and the District of Columbia; it was a land slide having earned his party 365 electoral votes. He only needed 270 electoral votes to win. Senator John McCain came in a distant second, in a two way race, having won 22 remaining states. He earned a paltry 173 Electoral states in the highly contested election. The campaign promise made by Senator Barack Obama during the early stages to reach out to all 50 states, did work in his party's favor, as many Republican strong holds otherwise referred to as the deep "Red" states started to turn purple, creating a very good opportunity for Democrats to win any of those states.

Many would argue that change was long coming to the US,

but the path to Barack Obama's victory was not as easy as it might appear today. Like many other observers of the process, I felt the nomination was Senator Hillary Clinton's for the asking, and by extension, - assessing the state of national issues and the looming economic problem, the presidency was hers'.

The Contest: Democrats

Barack Obama had to contest as an underdog in a very competitive and highly charged political process; he fought from a position of the underdog to become the front runner, as discussed in chapters 2 & 3.

Candidate Barack Obama's decision was to approach the entire campaign from the perspectives of the grassroots and from a principled stance. This demanded that issues should be the main point of discussion rather than personalities and fanfare, which had characterized prior election campaigns. It did a lot to force a sustained focus on matters that affected ordinary citizens and created a platform which he won his party's nomination and eventually the presidency.

Platform; Major Issues

Economy:

Barack Obama's positions on the economy, on the war in Iraq or other major issues were clear, unambiguous and well thought through. In 2002 he gave a speech on the decision by President Bush to invade Iraq. In it he was alert to the growing neglect of the real sector by focusing on perceived earnings and paper strength, of American companies. He did ask for greater oversight, and admonished the government to take more than passing interest in the health and performance of US firms and businesses. He did speak out for more regulations in the financial industry, warning that not regulating the sector may come to hurt the entire economy. He was quick to suggest that President Bush left the nation's economic progress to the Wall Street and diverted a significant portion of the nation's resources to the war in Iraq. He advocated that government should pay more attention to creating more sustainable jobs, so that average citizens may be able to put food on the table, pay their bills and work to keep their homes.

Senator Obama had reacted to the mortgage crises by demanding more openness in the way mortgages were closed. He was very vocal against the practice of subprime loans; he voiced his opinion about deceptive practices against seniors and those whose credit scores were very low. Those who normally would not qualify to own homes were being hurriedly approved for mortgages. These loans were structured as Adjustable Rate Mortgage (ARM), requiring only interest payments to be made for a certain period before the payment on Principal became due.

When Wall Street came crashing, he was one of the reasoned voices that called for calm. He opined that things were bad, but Americans can weather the storm, only if they were prepared to do some common sense hard work. He admonished everyone that the sitting President George Bush deserved support in fixing the economy. While he agreed that 'the buck stops at the President's table', he stated that there was enough blame to go round. He supported the plan by President Bush to fund the trouble banks through "Troubled Asset Relief Program" (TARP), to the tune of $700billion.

Housing Crisis:

Barack Obama was a very early critic of the mortgage industry's unfair and greedy practice. He was disturbed by the sub-prime loans that were made by mortgage companies to individuals who could not truly afford these loans. Many of these loans were structured to allow the borrower pay interest components for a period of time, usually termed Adjustable Rate Mortgage (ARM). These loans ballooned to a single payment, requiring full payment on the Principal and Interest elements. The option left for the borrower unable to repay the entire loan would be to refinance, something that was usually highly impracticable, leading to mortgage foreclosures.

He believed that the housing problem would have to be tackled the same way that Wall Street financial woes were dealt with; he proposed to tie the loss of homes to loss of jobs. Therefore it was necessary to make all efforts at helping homeowners keep their jobs, and assist the banks stay afloat. He also endorsed a proposal to fund a second "Economic Stimulus Package" of about $30 billion provided for this package, he would earmark $10 billion that would go towards a Foreclosure Prevention Fund. This fund would seek to attain dual purpose of helping home owners keep their home, but would also address the issue of faulty lending practices.

Jobs:

Barack Obama's bold plan to create new jobs placed emphasis on "green" jobs. He plans to add many semi- skilled and skilled jobs, by providing job training programs aimed at "green technologies". Many of these workers would be responsible for retrofitting homes with more energy efficient windows, doors and other energy efficient cooling and heating systems. He also plans to create a "Manufacturing Fund", which would be innovation focused. The fund is based on The Michigan 21st Century Jobs Fund, a state-level program that has awarded $125million to businesses with the most ingenious suggestions to create new jobs. Barack Obama and Joe Biden initiative on job creation will also invest $150 billion over a 10- year period to advance the next generation fuel infrastructure, as well as bio-fuels. He would encourage the development and production of newer and more fuel efficient cars.

War in Iraq:

In a speech that Senator Obama gave at Federal Plaza Chicago in 2002, he derided President Bush on his decision to invade Iraq; he likened the President's decision to fight in Iraq as effectively dropping the ball.

Barack Obama described a war against Iraq, at the very best a rush decision and a really dumb one. This is a country that, as Senator Barack Obama put it, was not in any position to threaten US, nor was there any evidence of Iraq's weapons of mass destruction. He reasoned that such a move would further alienate US from the rest of the Muslim world, thus creating more security issues, than the war was supposed to resolve. He argued for the continued and sustained attack on Taliban. He hoped that the President would focus on the war in Afghanistan to wipe out Osama Bin Laden and his warriors. He figured that a war against the Taliban which claimed responsibility for attack on US soil on September 11 2001 would be less difficult to justify than against a Muslim nation like Iraq that has not harmed Americans.

He accused the government of spending Hundreds of Millions of Dollars daily to prosecute the war in Iraq, instead of using these resources to fix many broken facilities and social services. When a bridge collapsed in Minneapolis, he was quick to point out government's lack of proper oversight in handling rehabilitation of existing facilities.

During the campaign Senator Barack Obama made it clear that he thought ending the war in Iraq was the right thing to do in order to make Americans safer, he promised to end the war within a scheduled timeline. Senator Clinton and many in the Republican Party who voted for the war thought he was naïve about national security issues and the prosecution of the war in Iraq. But to many, Barack Obama was considered a very intelligent person and a good listener who was not afraid to seek better alternative or counsel of professionals in economics and other fields.

Energy:

Senator Barack Obama was concerned that Americans were relying too much on oil imported from the Middle East and the level of consumption of such imported fuel. He was an advocate for alternative energy, demanding that US government lead the way in investing in alternative sources of energy. He suggested that Americans drove huge energy inefficient cars, but he advised that cars with less fuel consumption were the way forward. He proposed that American homes be energy efficient; homes should be rehabbed to fit them with more energy efficient doors and windows.

At a point during the party primaries, he spoke against a tax holiday for consumers. At a time, when all other contenders were advocating for a repeal of fuel tax on gasoline purchased at the pump. Senator Hillary Clinton and Senator John McCain had both requested the Federal government to suspend the tax paid when consumers buy gas at the pump, this was to relieve the burden of high gas prices, after prices rose nationwide to almost $5 per liter. His understanding of the issues was considered first class and his ability to deliver his message to the voters was adjudged impressive.

Health Care:

Even though many critics would give the credit of a Universal health care to the consistent efforts of Senator Edward Kennedy and Senator Hillary Clinton, it is noteworthy that Barack Obama was also a very early advocate of better, affordable and more efficient health care system. He often stated that his ailing mother on her sick bed, diagnosed with ovarian cancer, was more preoccupied with paying the medical bills than getting well. He had worked with other Senators in Illinois to provide health care coverage to the needy; he thus had a very good credential on health matters. On the national stage, he proposed a federal subsidy program that would encourage employers to offer health care to all their employees, at a cheaper and more affordable rate.

While he did not propose a compulsory or government mandated health care, Barack Obama proposed a National health insurance program for individuals, who may not have any health coverage and may not qualify for existing federal program, and provide for individuals younger than 25 years to be covered by their parents. He reasoned that savings of over $50billion to be made from rolling back President Bush tax cuts would pay for his program. He also planned to allow drugs determined to be safe from third world countries, to be sold in the US and repeal the ban that prevents the US from negotiating with drug companies.

Tax

Senator Obama was not enthusiastic about President Bush tax cut and made no secret about it. He promised to roll back these tax cuts, especially for the top 5 percent of the tax payers. He also promised tax break for 95 percent of middle class workers who earn below $250,000 per annum.

He planned to give a $3000 refundable tax credit to companies for each additional employee hired during 2009 and 2010. He would raise expensing limit for small businesses to $250,000and eliminate capital gains on taxes on investment made in small businesses. Senator Barack Obama would be called all sorts of names for suggesting a tax cut for the lower paid workers and repealing of tax cut for the top 5percent of the population. He took time to explain his plan to every audience patiently, asking them to visit his web site for more details.

Barack Obama Education and Public Service

Barack Obama's public service started when he worked as a community organizer in Chicago. He went on to Harvard Law School in 1988, where he was elected first African -American Editor of the Harvard Law Review. Obama graduated in 1991. He joined the law firm of Miner, Barnhill & Galland in Chicago as a Civil rights lawyer. He also taught at the University of Chicago.

Barack Obama joined his Chicago South Side Neighborhood Democrats in organizing for voters drive and elections. Five years after graduating from Harvard law school, he won an election into the Illinois Senate. In the year 2000 he made an unsuccessful attempt to unseat Congressman Bobby Rush, in an effort to become a US Representative from Illinois.

Undeterred, in November 2004 he made another attempt at Federal level, this time he ran for the Senate seat vacated by Illinois US Senator Peter Fitzgerald. He won comfortably in a hotly contested race, defeating Alan Keyes (Republican) by winning over 70% of the votes cast. He thus became the third

African -American elected to the US Senate after Re-construction.

He was known to have worked with both Republicans and Democrats in the State Senate, to pass legislation, regarding capital punishment and other issues bothering on defendant's right to fair hearing. These bi-partisan qualities saw him through his freshman days in the US Senate.

Just barely three years in the US Senate, on February 10th 2007, Barack Obama stood at Old State capitol,(where Abraham Lincoln had once addressed the nation on need for unity) he announced his bid for Presidency of the US.

Education

A very highly educated and intelligent man, his road to success was as diverse and colorful as his experience schooling at various institutions. At the age of six, with his new family, his biological father and his mother were divorced, and his mother had remarried to an Indonesian, Barack Hussein Obama started school in Indonesia, his new home. He returned later to live with his maternal grandparents in Hawaii, where he completed his elementary education and later graduated with honors from Punahou Academy.

After completing high school, he went on to study at the Occidental College in Los Angeles, from where he transferred two years later, to Columbia University New York where he graduated with a degree in Political Science in 1983.He soon went on to study law and graduated from Harvard School of Law. He authored two books, Dreams from my father in (1995) and Audacity of Hope (2006).

Iran

Barack Obama made it clear to all that cared to listen that his reach out was to the Jewish community, and that he remained a friend of Israel. He further stated that a nuclear Islamic Theocracy would not be allowed to own nuclear capability. Obama did unreservedly support the Israel's invasion of Lebanon in

2006 and recently, in 2007, sponsored Iran Sanctions Enabling Act. All these point to an unchanged policy towards Iran in substance of the official position of the US government.

Although Obama promised to open dialogue with the Iranian people, he wants the Iranian government to stop any activities on the nuclear program within a year or face more unfriendly actions from the US and its allies. He said that Iran's position does not make it a huge threat as that posed by the Soviet Union many years ago, and certainly not as large in size. It therefore made sense that since the US spoke to the Soviets, speaking to Iran was just following tradition of strong Presidents of US. In other words, Obama promised to engage friends and foes in dialogue.

Family

Barack Hussein Obama was born on August 4, 1961, to his mother Ann Stanley Dunham and his father Barack Obama sr., a black man of Luo ethnicity from Nyanza province, Kenya. His grand father was a domestic servant to the British, who taught his son herding goats, as he grew up.

Barack Obama's mother grew up in Wichita Kansas. Her father joined the service, when he left his job on oil rigs to fight in World War II, he marched across Europe in Patton's army. Her mother also worked for the service on a bomber assembly line. At the end of the war, both studied on GI bill, with the help of Federal Housing Program, bought a house and moved to Hawaii.

His father met his mother at East – West Center of the University of Hawaii at Manoa, later divorced her, when Barack was two years old. Barack Obama Sr. earned PhD degree from Harvard and returned home to Kenya. His mother then married Lolo Soetoro, another East-West Center student from Indonesia. Obama's half- sister Maya Soetoro–Ng was born in Indonesia. When Barack Obama returned to Hawaii from Indonesia, he was raised by his grandparents. He was especially fond of Toot (his grand mother) Madelyn Lee Dunham, who died two days before the elections of November 2 2008.

Barack Obama's grandmother

Madelyn Dunham was born Madelyn Lee Dunham on October 26, 1922 in Peru, Kansas, she was the eldest daughter of Rolla Charles Payne and Leona Belle Payne. She met her husband Stanley Armour Dunham in Wichita Kansas, the couple got married on May 5, 1940 and moved to Hawaii.

Madelyn got a job at the Bank of Hawaii and rose to become the Vice-President of the bank.

The popular mantra that one's friend is an indication of the person's inner reflections is true with Barack Obama and his wife Michelle Obama. Barack Obama met his wife Michelle, a brilliant and highly educated pretty lady, in 1989 when he worked as a summer associate at the law firm of Sidley & Austin in Chicago.

Obama has been a dedicated father opting to return home to his family during his days as a US Senator, rather than remain with colleague back in Washington DC for weekends. He demonstrated this love and affection for his family throughout the campaign.

The First Lady

The United States First Lady, Michelle Obama was born January, 17 1964 in Chicago to Frasier and Marian Robinson. Her father Frasier was a city pump operator and a Democratic precinct captain. When Michelle was born Marian, a Spiegel's secretary, stayed home to take care of her and her brother Craig.

Michelle and her brother were two very beautiful and intelligent children who skipped second grade due to their excellence. Both attended the prestigious Princeton University, where Michelle graduated cum Laude with a BA in sociology in 1985, after which she went to Harvard Law School and graduated in 1988.

Barack's persistence, dedication, focus and intelligent ways convinced Michelle, that he was the man for her. A few years later, the couple got married and was blessed with their daughters Malia in 1998 and Sasha later in 2001.

After her husband won the elections, she invited her mother Marian Robinson to come along with the first family to the White House; she said it would provide some sense of stability for this Chicago South Side's family. Her daughters, Malia and Sasha, were very fond of their grand mother. It was reported that her mother reluctantly agreed to go along with the first family.

What to expect:

In the next few chapters, the book goes on to describe and analyze the US Presidential primaries. It highlights how Barack Obama became a candidate, how he won the Democratic Primaries and eventually the Presidency. It would also show how John McCain won the Republican Party Presidential Primaries and how he lost the General Elections. The book also offers an insight into how Barack Obama's "Change we can believe in" was made possible, and presents a glimpse into selected Newspapers and Magazines endorsements of President Barack Obama before the General Elections.

Chapter 2

The US Presidential Primaries

The Presidential primaries were crowded, with political heavy weights and the regular politicians jostling for position and attention. The idea that the highest political job of all in the land could be theirs has always been too tempting for many politicians to ignore.

The all male Republican cast was not unusual. The Democratic Primaries was not also different in the large number of candidates, it was however different in the inclusion of two candidates of historical importance and significance. There was a very articulate and highly educated black man and a woman of equally distinguished credentials. How both Senators would shape the character and outcome of the presidential primary is profiled below, the outcome also shaped the general elections.

The Players: The Democratic Primaries

The list included Senator Hillary Clinton, a popular US Senator from the state of New York, former First Lady, Senator John Edwards, (former US Democratic Party Vice-Presidential nominee) who ran with Senator John Kerry in the ill fated 2004 Presidential contest. Senator Joe Biden, from Delaware, (high ranking member of the Senate foreign relations committee), Representative Dennis Kucinich, from Ohio State, Governor Bill Richardson and Senator Barack Obama from Illinois State.

I cannot say what exactly goes on in the minds of politicians but I do say the many whose career I have been fortunate to follow are a bunch of irrepressible optimists. A politician would talk of an idea even if he knows that it's almost impracticable, and would offer to make it practicable. If the polls say the opposite, then it must be ignored. That's where I find Obama slightly different. He said that he would not have to lose sleep if he lost the election. I find his guided utterances and how he deployed his political machinery quite interesting. He seemed to have mastered the art of being "cool", and learned to trust and to depend on those whom he believed could get the job done. Noted for his peculiar body language, his mild manners and combination of intelligence, determination and focus, he was able to build a formidable political machine. This machine initially did not appear to pose any threat but went on to reveal its ability as the campaign progressed.

No serious minded pollster initially gave Senator Obama a real chance. For many the parade that included him was just a show, the truth was that Senator Hillary Clinton was the unspoken "chosen one". I remembered being concerned that a handsome black senator from my state, who I thought had a promising future, in the US Senate, was being railroaded by some guided hands in the Democratic Party and even by non-party members. I thought there must be a plot to include a black man in the lineup for photo-op. I secretly wished and hoped that John Edwards would edge out Hillary Clinton. Her stand on the war in Iraq and hawkish positions on some issues of personal interest put me off her kind of politics. But as I listened to all the candidates speak during the debates, I began to really wish and hope that Barack Obama somehow made it to the convention.

Barack Obama and his team:

While all I could do was hoped, listened and watched events unfold; Obama and his campaign team took their intent very seriously. His team was managed by his Chicago friends and allies David Plouffe, and David Axelrod, and Robert Gibbs. Gibbs, former spokesman for Senator Kerry's Presidential campaign, was an experienced communications and campaign spokesperson, dating back 1998. Axelrod, a Chicago Democratic Party consultant had worked with Senator Edwards and Governor Vilsack prior to working with Obama. Plouffe the campaign manager was a partner in the consultant firm that ran Obama's 2004 senate race, he had served as a deputy chief of staff to Representative Gephardt.

The Davids ran a machine that reminded one of the stories of David against Goliath. They would think in small numbers. Just as the Goliath was defeated by a relatively untested person, the many names in the Democratic Party line up would fall. Many of the candidates were of the old guard, working from the first principles; they relied on name recognition, old favors and wads of cash to spend.

Barack Obama's 2004 Speech: Fresh Ideas

The equation did change a bit, Obama was not entirely unknown in the nation's political space, and indeed a speech he once gave at the Democratic Party's convention for Senator Kerry's Presidential nomination in Boston casted him into national political limelight. He had said "On behalf of the great state of Illinois, crossroads of a nation, land of Lincoln, let me express my deep gratitude for the privilege of addressing this convention. Tonight is a particular honor for me because, let's face it; my presence on this stage is pretty unlikely."

"My father was a foreign student, born and raised in a small village in Kenya. He grew up herding goats, went to school in a tin- roof shack. His father, my grandfather, was a cook, a domestic servant to the British. But my grandfather had larger dreams for his son. Through hard work and perseverance my father got a scholarship to study in a magical place, America, that's shown as a beacon of freedom and opportunity to so many who had come before him.

While studying here my father met my mother. She was born in a town on the other side of the world, in Kansas.

Her father worked on oil rigs and farms through most of the Depression. The day after Pearl Harbor, my grandfather signed up for duty, joined Patton's army, marched across Europe. Back home my grandmother raised a baby and went to work on a bomber assembly line. After the war, they studied on the GI Bill, bought a house through FHA and later moved west, all the way to Hawaii, in search of opportunity.

And they too had big dreams for their daughter, a common dream born of two continents.

My parents shared not only an improbable love; they shared an abiding faith in the possibilities of this nation. They would give me an African name, Barack, or "blessed," believing that in a tolerant America, your name is no barrier to success.

They imagined me going to the best schools in the land, even though they weren't rich, because in a generous America you don't have to be rich to achieve your potential.

They're both passed away now. And yet I know that, on this night, they look down on me with great pride.

And I stand here today grateful for the diversity of my heritage, aware that my parents' dreams live on in my two precious daughters.

I stand here knowing that my story is part of the larger American story, that I owe a debt to all of those who came before me, and that in no other country on Earth is my story even possible.

Tonight, we gather to affirm the greatness of our nation not because of the height of our skyscrapers, or the power of our military, or the size of our economy; our pride is based on a very simple premise, summed up in a declaration made over two hundred years ago: "We hold these truths to be self-evident, that all men are created equal that they are endowed by their Creator with certain inalienable rights, that among these are life, liberty and the pursuit of happiness."

That is the true genius of America, a faith in simple dreams, an insistence on small miracles; that we can tuck in our children at night and know that they are fed and clothed and safe from harm; that we can say what we think, write what we think, without hearing a sudden knock on the door; that we can have an idea and start our own business without paying a bribe; that we can participate in the political process without fear of retribution; and that our votes will be counted -- or at least, most of the time.

This year, in this election, we are called to reaffirm our values and our commitments, to hold them against a hard reality and see how we are measuring up, to the legacy of our forbearers and the promise of future generations.

And fellow Americans, Democrats, Republicans, independents, I say to you, tonight, we have more work to do, for the workers I met in Galesburg, Illinois, who are losing their union jobs at the Maytag plant that's moving to Mexico, and now they're having to compete with their own children for jobs that pay 7 bucks an hour; more to do for the father I met who was losing his job and chocking back the tears wondering how he would pay $4,500 a months for the drugs his son needs without the health benefits that he counted on; more to do for the young woman in East St. Louis, and thousands more like her who have the grades, have the drive, have the will, but doesn't have the money to go to college.

Now, don't get me wrong, the people I meet in small towns and big cities and diners and office parks, they don't expect government to solve all of their problems. They know they have to work hard to get a head. And they want to.

Go into the collar counties around Chicago and people will tell you: They don't want their tax money wasted by a welfare agency or by the Pentagon.

Go into any inner-city neighborhood, and folks will tell you that government alone can't teach kids to learn.

They know that parents have to teach, that children can't achieve unless we raise their expectations and turn off the television sets and eradicate the slander that says a black youth with a book is acting white. They know those things.

People don't expect -- people don't expect government to solve all their problems. But they sense, deep in their bones, that with just a slight change in priorities, we can make sure that every child in America has a decent shot at life and that the doors of opportunity remain open to all. They know we can do better. And they want that choice.

In this election, we offer that choice. Our party has chosen a man to lead us who embodies the best this country has to offer. And that man is John Kerry.

John Kerry understands the ideals of community, faith and service because they've defined his life. From his heroic service in Vietnam to his years as a prosecutor and lieutenant governor, through two decades in the United States Senate, he has devoted himself to this country. Again and again, we've seen him make tough choices when easier ones were available. His values and his record affirm what is best in us.

John Kerry believes in an America where hard work is rewarded. So instead of offering tax breaks to companies shipping jobs overseas, he offers them to companies creating jobs here at home.

John Kerry believes in an America where all Americans can afford the same health coverage our politicians in Washington have for themselves.

John Kerry believes in energy independence, so we aren't held hostage to the profits of oil companies or the sabotage of foreign oil fields.

John Kerry believes in the constitutional freedoms that have made our country the envy of the world, and he will never sacrifice our basic liberties nor use faith as a wedge to divide us.

And John Kerry believes that in a dangerous world, war must be an option sometimes, but it should never be the first option.

You know, a while back, I met a young man named Seamus (ph) in a VFW hall in East Moline, Illinois. He was a good-looking kid, 6'2", 6'3", clear eyed, with an easy smile. He told me he'd joined the Marines and was heading to Iraq the following week.

And as I listened to him explain why he had enlisted -- the absolute faith he had in our country and its leaders, his devotion to duty and service -- I thought, this young man was all that any of us might ever hope for in a child. But then I asked myself: Are we serving Seamus (ph) as well as he's serving us?

I thought of the 900 men and women, sons and daughters, husbands and wives, friends and neighbors who won't be returning to their own hometowns. I thought of the families I had met who were struggling to get by without a loved one's full income or whose loved ones had returned with a limb missing or nerves shattered, but still lacked long-term health benefits because they were Reservists.

When we send our young men and women into harm's way, we have a solemn obligation not to fudge the numbers or shade the truth about why they are going, to care for their families while they're gone, to tend to the soldiers upon their return and to never, ever go to war without enough troops to win the war, secure the peace and earn the respect of the world.

Now, Let me be clear. We have real enemies in the world. These enemies must be found. They must be pursued. And they must be defeated.

John Kerry knows this. And just as Lieutenant Kerry did not hesitate to risk his life to protect the men who served with him in Vietnam, President Kerry will not hesitate one moment to use our military might to keep America safe and secure.

John Kerry believes in America. And he knows that it's not enough for just some of us to prosper. For alongside our famous individualism, there's another ingredient in the American saga, a belief that we are all connected as one people.

If there's a child on the south side of Chicago who can't read, that matters to me, even if it's not my child.

If there's a senior citizen somewhere who can't pay for their prescription and having to choose between medicine and the rent that makes my life poorer, even if it's not my grandparent.

If there's an Arab-American family being rounded up without benefit of an attorney or due process that threatens my civil liberties.

It is that fundamental belief -- it is that fundamental belief -- I am my brother's keeper, I am my sisters' keeper -- that makes this country work.

It's what allows us to pursue our individual dreams, yet still come together as a single American family: "E pluribus unum," out of many, one.

Now even as we speak, there are those who are preparing

to divide us, the spin masters and negative ad peddlers who embrace the politics of anything goes.

Well, I say to them tonight, there is not a liberal America and a conservative America; there's the United States of America.

There's not a black America and white America and Latino America and Asian America; there's the United States of America.

The pundits, the pundits like to slice and dice our country into red states and blue States: red states for Republicans, blue States for Democrats. But I've got news for them, too. We worship an awesome God in the blue states, and we don't like federal agents poking around our libraries in the red states.

We coach little league in the blue states and, yes, we've got some gay friends in the red states.

There are patriots who opposed the war in Iraq, and there are patriots who supported the war in Iraq.

We are one people, all of us pledging allegiance to the stars and stripes, all of us defending the United States of America.

In the end, that's what this election is about. Do we participate in a politics of cynicism, or do we participate in a politics of hope?

John Kerry calls on us to hope. John Edwards calls on us to hope. I'm not talking about blind optimism here, the almost willful ignorance that thinks unemployment will go away if we just don't think about it, or health care crisis will solve itself if we just ignore it.

That's not what I'm talking. I'm talking about something more substantial. It's the hope of slaves sitting around a fire singing freedom songs; the hope of immigrants setting out for distant shores; the hope of a young naval lieutenant bravely patrolling the Mekong Delta; the hope of a millworker's son who dares to defy the odds; the hope of a skinny kid with a funny name who believes that America has a place for him, too.

Hope in the face of difficulty, hope in the face of uncertainty, the audacity of hope: In the end, that is God's greatest gift to us, the bedrock of this nation, a belief in things not seen, a belief that there are better days ahead.

I believe that we can give our middle class relief and provide working families with a road to opportunity.

I believe we can provide jobs for the jobless, homes to the homeless, and reclaim young people in cities across America from violence and despair.

I believe that we have a righteous wind at our backs and that as we stand on the crossroads of history, we can make the right choices and meet the challenges that face us.

America, tonight, if you feel the same energy that I do, if you feel the same urgency that I do, if you feel the same passion that I do, if you feel the same hopefulness that I do, if we do what we must do, then I have no doubt that all across the country, from Florida to Oregon, from Washington to Maine, the people will rise up in November, and John Kerry will be sworn in as president. And John Edwards will be sworn in as vice president. And this country will reclaim its promise. And out of this long political darkness a brighter day will come.

Thank you very much, everybody.

God bless you.

Thank you.

That was Barack Obama in 2004, the years passed by and his ideas still had freshness. As will be evident later, he worked hard to make the ideas more believable and realizable in 2008.

Democratic Primaries-Iowa's Choice:

Primary elections and caucuses, are an opportunity for a candidate to obtain enough delegates to the Party's National Convention. After tally of delegates, the candidate with the majority, represented the party in US general elections to elect the President. The very first test in the primaries was at Iowa on Jan5 2008.With a majority of white voters, Obama was not on the radar to make any impact, but his team knew he had to win Iowa, if he was to be taken seriously. Boy did he win? Here is the result at a glance, Obama had 940 votes representing about 38% of the total votes cast and 16 delegates, with John Edwards at second position with close to 30% of the votes cast with 344 votes and 14 delegates, coming a distant third was Hillary Clinton with 15 delegates, approximately 29% of the votes cast.

There was euphoria in the land for Obama's win, some called his win a landslide, while others shouted change, still others were dazed to a point that they felt this must be a Cinderella story. I remembered discussing with my brothers on the outcome; my two brothers in Nigeria were very pro Clinton and could not believe what had just happened. "He must have had the black votes" was their response. Wait a minute, I replied, that State had over 92% whites as voters.

"This is only a fluke then", they complained ceaselessly, when I reminded them that this was the United States of America, politics happens, change does happen, it maybe we were witnessing true change. Even his campaign was ecstatic, they had adopted a feel good song by Steve Wonder "Like a fool I went and stayed too long….. Oo baby, here I am, signed, sealed delivered, I'm yours… I could be a broken man but here I am with your future, got your future babe (here I am baby)

Here I am baby (signed, sealed delivered, I'm yours…"

Obama's team planned to create a new group of supporters to join the Democratic party base, while they worked to earn the trust of old ones. They smartly adapted Howard Dean's (Democratic Party Chairman) method of using the internet to raise money and awareness. Dean lost the Presidential primaries to Kerry in Iowa in 2004, but was very successful in raising cash from internet sources. That's all the team was to borrow from Dean; they understood how he lost Iowa, learned from his mistakes, and went on to win. To win Iowa, the team figured they had to develop new voters, independent and loyal party members alike. It went to town working behind the scenes and unknown to the Clinton's campaign team, registered new voters. Obama's team offered first time voters opportunities to partake and to own a process many rarely gave any thought about. To the young enthusiastic college students and fresh graduates, it was fun. They (the youth) felt they could connect with this "cool dude," who just might be their winning candidate as opposed to a party stalwart, who never bothered to connect. Never before was a generation so energized and involved in the decision making within a democratic process as was witnessed with this team.

Funding:

Money is to the politician what water is to the lost Bedouin in the desert, he must treat it with all the care in the world, not knowing when or if he would come across an oasis. Well, Obama and his team decided to map out several oases, even if these would be handfuls. They reasoned that if many people were to give in small amounts, but regularly, then they would cross the desert, with more than camel loads of treasure. They would likely outlast their opponents, whose reservoir was measured and determinate.

Yes they did, they ensured that Senator Clinton's camp spent heavily, took few prizes for their efforts; while they (Obama's team) cashed in commensurate to their pool of fund. I thought his major worry was the party's Super Delegates, who were pledged to Senator Clinton disproportionately from the onset. He did erase the deficit by a combination of deft reach- out to party elders and stalwarts, in a non-combative way, asked for their guidance even if he was not on their favored list. He created a subtle and sometimes not so subtle appeal about his initial and continued position on the ill advised Iraq war. This was the very Democratic Party's platform to criticize the Republicans.

Platform

Opposition to Iraq War

Since the Iraq war had been largely unpopular with Americans going to the primaries, Obama was seen as a fine party faithful. In the speech he gave at the Federal plaza in Chicago in 2002 he said; "I stand before you as someone who is not opposed to war in all circumstances. The Civil War was one of the bloodiest in history, and yet it was only through the crucible of the sword, the sacrifice of multitudes, that we could begin to perfect this union and drive the scourge of slavery from our soil.

I Don't Oppose All Wars

I don't oppose all wars. My grandfather signed up for a war the day after Pearl Harbor was bombed, fought in Patton's army. He fought in the name of a larger freedom, part of that arsenal of democracy that triumphed over evil.

I don't oppose all wars. After September 11, after witnessing the carnage and destruction, the dust and the tears, I supported this administration's pledge to hunt down and root out those who would slaughter innocents in the name of intolerance, and I would willingly take up arms myself to prevent such tragedy from happening again.

Opposed to Dumb, Rash Wars

I don't oppose all wars. What I am opposed to is a dumb war. What I am opposed to is a rash war. What I am opposed to is the cynical attempt by Richard Perle and Paul Wolfowitz and other armchair, weekend warriors in this administration to shove their own ideological agendas down our throats, irrespective of the costs in lives lost and in hardships borne.

What I am opposed to is the attempt by political hacks like Karl Rove to distract us from a rise in the uninsured, a rise in the poverty rate, a drop in the median income, to distract us from corporate scandals and a stock market that has just gone through the worst month since the Great Depression.

That's what I'm opposed to. A dumb war. A rash war. A war based not on reason but on passion, not on principle but on politics.

On Saddam Hussein

Now let me be clear: I suffer no illusions about Saddam Hussein. He is a brutal man. A ruthless man. A man who butchers his own people to secure his own power.... The world, and the Iraqi people, would be better off without him.

But I also know that Saddam poses no imminent and direct threat to the United States or to his neighbors...and that in concert with the international community he can be contained until, in the way of all petty dictators, he falls away into the dustbin of history.

I know that even a successful war against Iraq will require a U.S. occupation of undetermined length, at undetermined cost, with undetermined consequences.

I know that an invasion of Iraq without a clear rationale and without strong international support will only fan the flames of the Middle East, and encourage the worst, rather than best, impulses of the Arab world, and strengthen the recruitment arm of al-Qaeda.

I am not opposed to all wars. I'm opposed to dumb wars. So for those of us who seek a more just and secure world for our children, let us send a clear message to the president.

You Want a Fight, President Bush?

You want a fight, President Bush? Let's finish the fight with Bin Laden and al-Qaeda, through effective, coordinated intelligence, and a shutting down of the financial networks that support terrorism, and a homeland security program that involves more than color-coded warnings.

You want a fight, President Bush? Let's fight to make sure that...we vigorously enforce a nonproliferation treaty, and that former enemies and current allies like Russia safeguard and ultimately eliminate their stores of nuclear material, and that nations like Pakistan and India never use the terrible weapons already in their possession, and that the arms merchants in our own country stop feeding the countless wars that rage across the globe.

You want a fight, President Bush? Let's fight to make sure our so-called allies in the Middle East, the Saudis and the Egyptians, stop oppressing their own people, and suppressing dissent, and tolerating corruption and inequality, and mismanaging their economies so that their youth grow up without education, without prospects, without hope, the ready recruits of terrorist cells.

You want a fight, President Bush? Let's fight to wean ourselves off Middle East oil through an energy policy that doesn't simply serve the interests of Exxon and Mobil.

Those are the battles that we need to fight. Those are the battles that we willingly join. The battles against ignorance and intolerance, corruption and greed, poverty and despair."

The road to Minneapolis:
New Hampshire Primaries

Pollsters gave the much prized New Hampshire caucuses to Obama- I don't understand the noise over four delegates; fact, I am not a politician. On the eve of the election, his campaign song was on every air wave, prematurely celebrated another win. He got it wrong this time; he lost to a weeping Hillary Clinton. This loss would be explained by many as "Bradley effect"- this happens, when a white voter would say one thing about voting for a black candidate and does otherwise. As far as I was concerned, I think the voters suddenly turned to Hillary Clinton after she sought attention by breaking down in public space; here was a woman whose nerves were supposedly made of steel. Barack learnt his lessons like all successful people do, never be unmindful of possible pitfall.

He nearly fell off the bus at one of his exploratory meetings, the previous year in South Carolina. After he almost lost his crowd by unrelated remarks, an old lady gave him his mojo back, when she shouted "..Are you fired up and ready to go..?" He quickly latched on to that phrase, as he would continue to light up his crowd, supporters after supporters and one campaign stop after another, he would never look back, even as Senator Clinton was breathing down his neck.

Super Tuesday

Senator Hillary Clinton had banked her hopes on Super Tuesday, a day in which majority of the states 24 in total, including U.S. Pacific territory of American Samoa went to the polls. It represented the largest single voting day in the nomination process; it did little to help rout Barack Obama. Even though she earned more delegates to stay in the race, she did not garner enough delegates' counts to stop this rising star.

To win on this extra ordinary night, her campaign resorted to all manners of politicking, including throwing the kitchen sink at Obama. At a point she called for a 3:00 am phone call from the pro-war state of Texas, a deeply conservative outlet. Though the phone calls or lack of them did hurt Obama in some counties in Texas, he only dusted his Jacket to brush aside any signs of disrespect. He taught Clinton a lesson or two in staying awake for the 3.00am call; she won the delegates count but lost the caucus.

All manners of wrenches thrown in the wheels of change by the Clinton's team were quickly addressed in such a clinically efficient manner. It irritated the Republicans so much, that media attention was tuned to these two giants slugging it out in the open field. Their own candidate Senator McCain, crowned in a swift manner, was hardly noticed in the media. To be fair, the media seemed to have been in a kind of darling romance with Obama. Oprah Winfrey was not alone in the dream world of an Obama presidency, the rest of the entertainment world, including majority of networks with notable exception of Fox channel, and a host of other conservative Media houses were living the dream story.

During the primaries and general elections campaign, Senator Obama pulled crowd of supporters, never seen in recent US history of campaigning, in places like St Louis, Minneapolis, Miami and host of others, he was a true American political star.

Check out the formal results when Senator Clinton threw a sledge hammer at her opponent in Ohio, unscrewed his gas cap in Michigan, created a bottle neck in Pennsylvania and finally tossed him outside in the tropical rains of Florida. Even Turbaning Hussein and Islamizing Barack Obama on the campaign trail, only served to empower him when he conceded with a douse of humor to "reject and denounce" Minister Farrakhan's word. Senator Clinton had demanded him to say he "rejected" Farrakhan's words, even after Senator Obama offered to "denounce" the Minister (She felt "reject" was a stronger term than "denounce"). The total delegates won after Florida and Michigan got full seating and Super Delegates voted were a story on its own; with both candidates locked in battle and bitter rancor over who got what and who won these states. The 2 states were suspended for shifting their primary elections dates without full permission from the party's national committee– Obama; pledged delegates 1763, Super delegates 438, giving him a total of 2201 delegates compared to Clinton's 1640 pledged delegates and Super delegates of 256 making a total of 1896 voting delegates.

The result through the end of June 2008 was representative of the appreciation of the efforts put in by the candidates from fall 2007 through summer 2008. Straight to the conventions in August with a dream ticket of Barack Obama and Joe Biden, a decision that brought joy to millions of Independents, Democrats and some reform minded Republicans

The Republican Presidential Primaries

The line up of the candidates for the chance to represent the Party in November 2008 general elections was impressive but not colorful as it was predictable. Governor Mitt Romney, Governor Mike Huckabee, Senator Sam Brownback, Mayor Rudy Giuliani, Senator Fred Dalton Thompson, Rep Duncan Hunter, Rep Ron Paul and Senator John McCain, who was endorsed by majority of the candidates after one poor showing or the other.

What many considered impressive was the presence of die hard conservative party faithful like Governor Mike Huckabee, Mormon devout Governor Mitt Romney and Mayor Rudy Giuliani. All of them were thought to be successful administrators and tough on twin issues of crime and homeland security. But with several marital and family issues that wrestled Giuliani, including allegations of financial imprudence, he missed out in Florida. It was his only shot at getting some real traction, he dropped out and endorsed McCain. Irreconcilable differences between the Christian right wing of the Party put paid to Governor Romney's bid, he later endorsed McCain. Someone many thought was exciting to have on the ballot in November was Mike Huckabee, but his brand of hard line right wing evangelist politics also appeared to have alienated others in the Party. He remained long enough in the race to keep the Republican Party primaries news worthy.

What I found most disturbing was that the conservatives, whom many observers thought had fine gentlemen and brilliant ideas to reinvent themselves, fell into a serious trap of identity crises. The party was a victim of several elections successes in the recent past, which were now being mismanaged. Many party adherents were too busy looking to the top hierarchy composed of older graying white men, for salvation of the party. America is a multi racial, multi-religious society, a serious organization cannot hope to claim political leadership, by creating fear of one section of the society against the other. Muslims, who normally voted in large numbers for the conservatives, were maligned by the Bush policies and derided by many commentators for the Republican Party, many issues that were debated by the Republicans were no longer debatable. Many young conservatives had no outlet to vent their frustrations, caustic Republican Talk show hosts became spokespersons for the Party. These disillusioned members, either voted Barack Obama in the elections or refrained from voting entirely. Splinters in the Party, including crisis of leadership may have contributed to the manner in which candidates got dropped, resulting in a candidate by endorsement; Senator John McCain.

How the African Americans Voted

I spoke with many of my friends in the African American communities, mostly those from Nigeria, West Africa and North Africa about their views as the events unfolded. I wanted to gauge their feelings and to find out how they would likely vote. The result was stunning, majority of those I spoke to favored Senator Hillary Clinton to win the nomination as Presidential flag bearer for the Democratic Party. These people said they remembered that "times were good", under President Bill Clinton and it would only get better under a future "President Hillary Clinton". I advised them to give Barack Obama a chance, by listening to what he had to say. I invited them to discuss the issues.

High on the list of issues for many of us from Africa were Education, Economy, and the War in Iraq and African affairs. On the Economy, the votes were skewed on the higher side about 65 percentage points for Senator Clinton. While Obama scored slightly higher almost 55 percentage points on Education, majority about 80 percentage points went for him on the War in Iraq. Senator Clinton scored very high over 85 percentage points when it came to who would care most about Africa. The demographics also presented another interesting way to review the support for both candidates. About eight out of ten women supported Clinton's bid, the men split their support seven out of ten for Obama's bid. These voters preference for the candidates would persist past the Iowa caucus result, and spilled over to Super Tuesday.

The grounds began to shift significantly in favor of Barack Obama, when Clinton's campaign began to attack her opponent in very negative tones. For many African Americans, the attacks were personal. Reference to Obama's non- appeal to "hard working blue collar whites", was off the mark. That statement only reinforced the stereotypical views of the white man- that average black man was lazy. My community may not be regarded as lazy; these are well educated, smart and hardworking people, who denounced any form of negative stigma. The men felt insulted, for most African men, husbands are the head of the family. Any attempt to ridicule him, especially by a woman is viewed in extreme negative form. Obama had fulfilled the perfect role of a father and a husband; he was therefore not to be rubbished by Clinton. They moved enmasse towards Obama. The women on the other hand were not so offended, it was sort of liberating for most of Clinton's supporters. Many of these women later voted Obama only after Senator Clinton conceded.

Chapter 3

The Man: Barack Hussein Obama

Barack Obama was born in Honolulu, Hawaii in 1961. His parents met there while in college. His father was from Kenya and his mother from Wichita, Kansas. They divorced when he was only 2 years old. While still in college, his mother met another student from Indonesia. The couple got married and moved to Jakarta in 1967 where Barack attended local schools. In 1971, Obama returned to Hawaii to live with his maternal grandparents. There he attended a college preparatory school until his graduation from high school in 1979. He said that as a young adult he struggled with strong feelings concerning his multi-racial heritage, but believed that growing up in Hawaii where there were many cultures aided his understanding and ultimately became an integral part of his world-view.

Obama's run for presidency of the United States came at an opportune time in US history. His forthright approach to the serious issues that had taken the life out of the US economy proved to be enough, in spite of many challenges from respected candidates and seasoned politicians. He was viewed as an underdog, considering the high profile list of Democrats like Senator Hillary Clinton, Senator Joe Biden, and Senator John Edwards; he has now emerged as an historic figure, the first African American to become President of the United States of America.

During his campaign, all manners of lies and guilt by association were thrown his way; he was accused of faking his belief, charges were that he was of the Islamic faith. Something he denied, but worked to point out that there was nothing wrong for an American to be a Muslim, he made no secret of the faith being part of his larger family, especially in Kenya. Photographs of his visit to Africa wearing traditional garments were displayed as if he was a warrior of the African descent; quick response by his campaign team doused the fire of controversy. Still it was announced that he had attended a madrassa for Islamic youth, even as the perpetrators of the untrue were aware of the facts. At another junction, his very practice of Christianity was examined and questioned; big story was made about an old friend and Pastor of his church, Jeremiah Wright who many believed held some radical views in certain areas. In spite of all these setbacks and potential career-threatening obstacles, Barack Obama held a strong lead over McCain for most of the political race.

Road map to Change we can believe in

The coming of black people to America in the early days (1619 to 1865) was mainly through forced displacement from their fatherland, in the harsh form of slavery and slave trade. The evils of slavery and slave traders are beyond the scope of this book. My intention is to show how emancipation of slaves through the times and the struggle for recognition of the contributions of these slaves and their progeny to the present day happenings in America and the world in general. The thawing of master slave relationship was a long struggle by many black men and women, who themselves were either slaves who bought their freedom, or of those who fled the inhuman treatment. Of these are Frederick Douglas, W.E.B. Du Bois and Harriet Tubman.

Many tools were employed by the dominant group, the whites to keep the minority group the blacks, from gaining political power or becoming economically independent. All forms of discriminations were meted out to the average black person; there was deliberate avoidance of persons of brown skin in congregational settings, places of work and recreation, including institutions of education. There was also State sponsored exclusion of able bodied black persons from legitimate means of economic and political advancement. Countless incidences of police brutality and torture of black people were supported actively by the establishment, including unfortunately the judicial system. Individuals and law enforcement routinely carried out massacre of black for the simplest excuse with little or no reprimand.

Minority groups response to prejudice & discrimination

Vast majority of historians situate the genesis of the new movement for civil rights in the United States to the incidence which happened in Montgomery, Alabama when a black woman Rosa Parks, an unknown seamstress, would not give up her seat for a white person. Her insistence to remain seated in a 3 person arrangement, after 2 black men had given up their seats for 1 white man, led to her arrest and fine for violation of a city ordinance. On December 1 1955, this single act of courage and bravely in the face of legal consequence, led to organized movement to defy the laws of segregation, resulting in Montgomery Bus Boycott. An unrelenting and constant call for more freedom and right of participation by many blacks, aided by a sizeable number of whites and other concerned minority groups, developed into what is termed the freedom march on Washington.

The march which took place in 1963 was organized by Bayard Rustin, A. Philip Randolph, John Lewis, Martin Luther King, Roy Wilkins and Whitney Young. The original initiative was that of Randolph, who was responsible for planning a similar march in 1941. It was here that MLK gave his famous I have a dream speech, the outcome of the march, a brilliant outing by MLK and the team, gave rise to Civil Rights Act (1964) and subsequently the National Voting Rights Acts (1965).

The dream of MLK that one day his sons and daughters would be judge by their character and not by the color of their skin, was not going to remain a dream, many blacks knew what they were up against, but only a few men would be prepared to stake their reputation and intelligence to advance the course of their kith and kin in politics.

Early success in a political race was achieved by Shirley St Hill Chisholm, who in 1964 ran for the New York state assembly seat, she also made it to the US Congress by 1968 and was re-elected for a second term by 1970. She was credited with a lot of progress in women and minority affairs, actively campaigning for the betterment of the woman folk, she announced her candidacy for Presidency in 1972 at the Democratic Party Convention in Miami, becoming the first woman and a black person of any major party considered for nomination as a Presidential candidate.

Twelve years later, in 1984, Jesse Jackson ran as a Democrat for the office of the President, he was placed third in a race that saw Walter Mondale became the Presidential candidate. Not deterred by his low delegate count, about 8% of the total delegates, he ran for the office again in 1988 and put up a better showing. About twenty years after Jackson ran Obama took the stage in 2004 at the Democratic convention for John Kerry and made his famous speech about a United States of America, where there were no Red states and or Blue states, but a people united by common goals. The stage was being set; a powerful orator was in the making; many commentators actually predicted he was going to displace President Clinton, as one of the best orators the party had.

When Obama got his chance in the sun, he made very good use of it. He did not come across as a civil rights activist nor was he considered an angry black man. He came across in the political scene to many in the Democratic Party as one of their rising stars. It is easy for anyone of us to gloat over Obama's victory at the polls on November 4th 2008, making him the first black man to occupy the highest office of the land. Many would want us to believe what made it possible was his intelligence, his charm, the message of change, including the campaign strategy adopted by his team. Still others would add his "cool" temperament got him on the side of majority. While some would have Americans thank Bush for giving US Obama, citing the failed war in Iraq, spying on and wire tapping defenseless citizens. Yet there are some who would say that Mc-Cain would have won, were it not for the melt down of Wall Street and near collapse of the entire financial system. These commentators were quick to point out that McCain was leading in the polls, right after he announced Sarah Palin as his running mate, only to see a decline in fortune when the Wall Street brouhaha erupted. Sarah Palin's divisive politics, is the way of the Republican elections success, many conservatives would agree, they talk of red meat, use slangs like anti- God to slander their opponent. For sure the scare tactics worked for the Republicans against candidates who, were either too timid to confront them, or rather slow to respond or even those who try to imitate them at their game.

If you were timid, you looked weak in the eyes of the unsuspecting electorates, many voters were bamboozled, and confused so much that they would turn their gaze away from what mattered most in elections- the issues. The talking point was either "soft on crime" or "soft on defense". Many Americans have been made to believe for a long time that until they go to war, they were weak. Some Republicans have started to analyze how Barack Obama's election blitz happened. Some of them have written their own side of the story, citing issues like grumpy old white men's party, loss of demographics- educated white men, upscale white women, blacks, Hispanics and Asians. Recently also many have mentioned the "Huxtable" (Bill Cosby 70's black family comedy show) effect to counter the "Bradley" effect

I do agree that no one factor may have been solely responsible for the seeming ease with which many Caucasians voted for Obama. However, I find it rather curious and strange that most commentators failed to acknowledge that these qualities namely; being an intellectual, charming, soft spoken or even cool looking, are not exactly sole premise of Barack Obama as a black man. Many black men, who possessed these qualities, in nearly a quarter of a century ago, could not go far enough. I think critical to Obama's win, is the ingredient of timing that allowed for all these fine qualities to be desired and sought by the average US voter, over color of skin or race. The country had come of age in an era of change, an era largely dominated by Oprah Winfrey on the one hand, even if subtly, and politicians with the greedy Wall Street players on the other.

The politicians in the last decade, have created a nation of "you are either for me or against me", a cowboy mentality. Divisive rhetoric was the order of the day; many gains of civil rights movement were rolled back in the name of angry white man politics. Many students were dropped by the bus stop, left behind by a policy that mouthed much but delivered nothing. The law makers encouraged executive lawlessness in the name of majority control, gave nod to a war that was obviously ill timed and at best unwise, these actions made many citizens distrust their leaders. On the other end, was subtle but relentless campaign by Oprah Winfrey a black woman, who used the entertainment medium to attend to daily concerns of the individuals, her audience was as diverse as the nation. On Oprah's daily show, she would speak to her audience with a sense of belonging, and with a common place intelligence, that provided comfort to her fans world wide. Oprah provided help to professionals trying to build on their careers, she invited professionals to advice her audience on wide ranging issues that affect the ordinary and the not so ordinary. And in the last decade, Oprah became a force to be reckoned with. Without political power or designated constituency, she made the world of Americans her constituency, created for herself and her fans enormous influence.

A dichotomy was created unnoticed, while the politicians went about their businesses, alienated their constituencies, the audience on Oprah's platform was consistently being energized to reason and to demand change in every facet of their lives. The influence of Oprah did not go unnoticed; the media was alive to it. Such was the suggestion that she should run for the exalted office of the President. Although she acknowledged the good intention of those who recommended her, she was aware of her limitations in the realm of politics, she was without an established political party base. Yet even as she commanded respect and followership across political divides, she would have to "belong", or join one of the two parties. To run as an Independent candidate may be too expensive even for Ms Winfrey. Many people questioned if the solutions to the country's problems were achievable through active partisanship or collaborative effort for change. These persons in their millions envisioned Oprah, not as a black woman, but as the force behind many positive acts. Several persons who felt she had the qualities to unite US began active calls for her to run for the office US President. The entrenched racial consideration- an unspoken dictum that a black person could not lead US, eventually did benefit Barack Obama in his quest for the White House.

Obamanation

Obamanation was a term coined by some of his supporters in apparent reference to his call for change, a demand for better politics that would lead to a unified nation. A call for blurred line between red states and blue states, a nation of people, who share common values and dream common goals. A nation driven by hope not held back by fear, a nation where all men are not only said to be born equal but are truly equal, where the limits are individually defined, not arbitrarily sponsored by the state. Hope for a nation that appreciates its' diverse cultures and honor its' commonalities. Central to the core of Obamanation philosophy is the commitment to give back to the community through acts of selfless service. He is also a committed faith- based solutions supporter, having witness the efforts of many churches in Chicago, to assist their communities in delivering the goods

Oprah Winfrey endorsed Obama, on Larry King live September 25 2006- through a suggestion that Obama should run for the office of the President. While she responded to a question about her own ambition, she put forward at risk her integrity, and business. Oprah, who had not before endorsed any Presidential candidate, risked being called names, black, and racially biased. She knew what might follow, especially by the conservative right wingers. She was after all the darling of everyone, Blacks, Whites, Asians, and Hispanics. How come now, why this person of her likeness? Questions did fly from everywhere you could imagine. Yes the questions came from all quarters, but a defiant and confident Oprah attended to these suggestions with intelligent responses. She was no push-over; standing by her were many other persons of diverse persuasions, who were on the Obama for President Train. They recognized what many others would later appreciate about the young Senator from Illinois, who always quoted Abraham Lincoln, who once fought for unity of US, a Senator and a great US, President, in his run for the White House.

A deliberate strategist herself, with an acute sense of self preservation, she indicated that she knew the person of Sen. Obama, and was therefore endorsing him. As she had endorsed good ideas on her shows .She said he was a personality, who could truly be trusted and relied upon by millions of Americans to bring the needed change,. She more than most people understood the effect of audience disaffection and what is described in politics as, 'voter turn around'- comparable only to buyer's remorse, but she felt good about her decision. By putting her name out there behind Sen. Barack Obama, Oprah Winfrey began the ground swell of organized grass root support in the public space, an upbeat effort by communities, to start the questions sessions, and toy with the idea of a black family in the white house .

The last decade can be said to be the beginning of Oprah Winfrey's era in entertainment, many people had come to love her as a intellectual talk show host. Her show was received as the go- to media shop; she was seen as a woman who had come of age, successful, compassionate and to many also down to earth. Oprah Winfrey can be credited with the groundswell of shift in opinion, about the power of the women folk, the place of reasoned solution in talk shows and the height to which a dedicated person may rise. Oprah to many people in the US and the world over, identified with a lot of good causes. Oprah's show promoted unity of purpose amongst her followers and fans. Her show helped to break barriers for a lot people, many of them black. These people opened their homes to her out of love. Oprah asked her viewers to amend their ways, make little changes to their life styles, stay healthy and have a chance to live longer. If Ms Winfrey spoke about beef, Texas would go bare; if she was to discuss cheese, Wisconsin would thaw, such was the power of persuasion Oprah had over airwaves. Oprah elicited a high level of audience excitement and arguably fiercely independent intellectual followership, rarely displayed by TV viewers in US and the world over. She had commanding numbers across the aisle. Comparison could be drawn of Obama and his followers, who were excited about the viability of their candidate, pleased at the sight of him, and attentive to his whispers, just check out Obama girl video on youtube .com.

During the primaries, as with the general elections campaign, Sen. Obama panned out the small caucus states, he earned votes enough to give him edge in delegate count, Obama knew how to strike, un-beknowest to the opponent. This strategy was akin to that employed by Muhammad Ali in his days of championship boxing. Ali, as he was popularly known, took his opponent through the rigors of boxing ring, he absorbed punches; threw effective jabs in a quick methodical way to weaken his opponent, enough to deliver a winning blow. While Obama took in punches from Clinton on Super Tuesday, California, and Massachusetts (hurts…Kennedy zone), New York and New Jersey, he landed a few very effective jabs of his own. By winning delegates in these states including in Texas; he gathered enough delegates in these states to remain competitive.

Obama's strategy was to rely on his experience as a community organizer as the key to remaining in play. The strategy to Muhammad Ali's wins was his resilience, and determination to go the extra distance, put his opponent under both physical pressure, and mental strain. Then to create doubt and confusion in his opponent's mind. While he planned, analyzed and appraised his chances, he went for every opportunity. He kept his opponents weak and without a winning strategy. When the opponents became weak or frustrated, they slowly let down their guards and committed errors, Muhammad Ali then threw his knock out punch. Obama's resilience and that of his campaign team came to play, after strings of losses on Super Tuesday; he had his next moves planned. He went on to earn the next set of delegates, in a way that left his opponents' camp counting their eggs, he held on to the basket. Anger, confusion and frustration enveloped the Clinton's campaign, as the results became more unfavorable to their candidate. The anointed had become vulnerable; the threat was from a rookie. It brought home an uncomfortable reality, change may indeed happen. The Clinton campaign began to chew on each other, privately and publicly, campaign staffers were reassigned, some fresh faces were brought in to manage the campaign. When the Super Tuesday sweep strategy failed to work, Clinton camp devised new tactics. The camp let loose some of her surrogates to run wild, with stories about Obama in African warrior regalia, and of him being a madrassa (Islamic) scholar, including when convenient, the dirty race card. All in the hope to raise the fear of electability, and to create doubts about an Obama candidacy, thus rejecting change.

Hillary Clinton found herself under physical strain, she tried to belong in many ways; at some point she gobbled cups of beer to prove she belonged. Her campaign team were put under immense mental strain; they decided to throw all manners of kitchen sink at Mr. Obama. She even challenged him to try and catch her at winning the "hard- working blue collar whites" votes, a demographic that posed a headache for the change team. The percentage of votes that went his way from the white women was also a bit of concern. But the change team began to chart a viable course of action to grab this section once the primaries were done with. They figured many would face reality, what was at stake was beyond petty party squabbles- Supreme Court justices; Rowe Vs Wade, Affirmative action, Equal pay, and a host of others. In addition to all these losses, her campaign was burning cash fast. Their strategy to go for the short haul, against a long haul strategy of Barack Obama, was evidently short sighted, ill planned and did prove fatal.

Obama responded in his usual" Mr. Cool' approach, the" I would not join you in the mud fight," kind of attitude, focused more on his strategy. He understood what was not done correctly in any loss and primed up for the next round. After the loss of Ohio, Texas and Pennsylvania, Obama's' response was to pick up the very difficult state of North Carolina. He earned more Super Delegates, while Clinton, despite her wins, bled cash and lost a number of Super delegates. Hillary Clinton and Barack Obama did make their cases to an impatient, and nervous gathering of party elders, who were then perturbed that the tone of negative campaign may cost the party victory at the General Elections. Obama came out of these meetings, as he did come of the last primaries debate with Clinton, more victorious and definitely more Presidential.

During the campaign, Barack Obama's campaign team made it crystal clear that they would not entertain any smear campaign against their candidate. They responded swiftly with massive media blitz. More importantly, any reference to his wife on the campaign trail was out of bounds. He considered any attacks on his wife as "taking the low road," he was not prepared to join anyone on the low road, thus he effectively extinguished any hope of smear campaign on Michelle. Often for the reason of financial burden, quasi political associations called the 527's were employed to do the dirty job. The swift boat ad by Bush supporters was effective against John Kerry, even as it was acknowledged to be fabrications with malicious intent. Some rumors of Obama being Muslim- as if being a Muslim was anti American, were distributed but were quickly rebutted, there were other aimless talk of banning guns- something almost impossible due to strong gun lobby.

To present a formidable candidate for any election in the US, usually a campaign manager did more than the conventional marketing, especially when his candidate had to contest against Republican opponent. He would have to be schooled in the science of rebuttal and counter attack lunched by 527's. Because the Republicans tend to have more rich spoilers in their camp, a candidate under attack from conservative 527 supporters had a daunting task. Such was the task David Plouffe, Barack's campaign manager was saddled with. The war of words between the Democratic Party and the Republican Party, about which party was responsible for the sorry state of the economy and the bungled Iraq war, was frightening.

Many aides are required by campaign teams to manage communications for their candidate. Experienced assistants worked hard to present their candidates to the voters in the best manner they could. These professional advisers tended to study the mood of the voters and kept a close ear to the ground on every piece of information that may be of political importance. These pieces of information, usually of some significance, may be a negative piece of information on an opponent, or it may be a positive comment on their candidate. Schooled in the art of spin, the conservative advisers were quick to go to town, distributed misinformation on Obama's tax plan. First it was that he would raise taxes on all Americans earning $45k and above, when the Obama team responded with more openness and clarity. The story shifted to calling him a communist, they (the Republicans) accused him of planning to give tax cuts to non-working lower income- effectively taking from the tax payers and doling it out as welfare to the poor. This again was denied vehemently and a counter campaign was launched by the Obama team to dispel the rumors

In order to win elections, candidates believe they have to be seen first by their party base as "electable". In the process of getting this done, McCain's camp worked hard to sell their candidate to the party base as a true conservative. It may have included his choice of Governor Sarah Palin as Vice-Presidential candidate; she was really a fresh face in the boring McCain camp. Her selection, served as an early boost to his campaign as he stepped out of the Republican Party's Convention. However, the curiosity to get to know Ms Sarah Palin and the campaign's sequestration of the candidate, created doubts about her ability to step to the plate. Voters wanted to know who 'the heartbeat away' from the presidency was. Finally after she granted interviews, the much expected media love turned sour. The very moment she opened her mouth and responded to the series of questions reserved for kindergarten politicians, she bombed. Simple questions on ABC news network on President Bush's doctrine made matters worse. She knew nothing of the world as was expected of anyone who sought to step in the role of the President. Worse still, she came across as very plain and unintelligent to most observers. Her comments of seeing Russia from her window came across as lacking in foreign affairs and her inflamed rhetoric on the dispute between Russia and Georgia was considered cold war era politics. Despite all of these many of her supporters were upset about how Ms Palin was being assessed, they made a lot of noise about her executive experience and knowledge, but when she bungled questions related to what daily newspapers she read, she came across as less educated and even less prepared than her paper certification portended.

However, Barack's choice of Joe Biden as a running mate on the other hand, was well received by, conservatives and liberals alike as a wise decision. This singular action casted Obama in a better light than his opponent, Biden was seen as a plus for his experience in foreign affairs and his history of bipartisan dealings.

The McCain's campaign handlers felt that he needed to speak to his base, they made certain that his campaign position on most issues were a complete volte face of his earlier stance in US Senate. After opposing Bush's tax cuts earlier before the campaign, he turned around to support the tax cuts during his campaign. Those about -turns he made, were performed to make his so- called core constituency more comfortable with him. By contrast, Obama was consistent in his message; he offered tax cut for 95% of the working families who earned $250k and below. He also continued to press for regulation of the financial industry especially as it affected mortgage financing. A position McCain opposed for the duration of Bush's two terms until the financial melt down, when he called for sacking of Chris Cox as President of the SEC, a flub at best, before he began to join the call for regulation.

The decisions to do or say what was considered politically correct, or popular, by candidates may sometimes pay off, but can sometimes scare off voters; it remained a big gamble for most politicians. McCain and Clinton bought the bait; they both called for a gas tax holiday, during the primaries, when the price of gas went through the roof. The duo caught a serious populist bug that was not to be, the voters saw through the nonsense, and gave Obama his victory over a populist Clinton in North Carolina. Attempts to discredit Obama as an elitist was discountenanced by the general public, who would not be fooled by voodoo economics, they rooted for him to lead the nation by voting for him in large numbers.

Many commentators argued that for a politician the element of trust is essential; if the voters trust a candidate more than his opponent; he was more likely to win. Other factors that affected US voter's decision included how they assessed a candidate on the issue of national security, and if they considered him likeable enough. This is so because, when voters liked a candidate more than his opponent, the better liked is usually more trusted, that could determine his success at the polls. The message from a campaign manager was probably; that as long as his candidate was likeable, then the issue of trust was almost settled. Often a lot of pressure is endured to present the candidate from a "likeable" angle. The branding of a candidate is more often than not wrapped around the issue of likeability; a weapon used quite readily by the conservative politicians to their advantage. If their candidate did not pull enough likeability factors, the option was to chew on their opponents till the opponents are disliked. Sarah Palin was called out to do the damage, she shouted herself hoarse. She claimed Obama was a socialist, suggested doubts about his patriotism by rising suspicions about his person and his friends, but the people were not about to be fooled. The responses of Obama team to any disrespectful suggestions or statements were to refute these with intelligent rebuttal and dignified denial.

McCain's decision to pick Sarah Palin as his running mate, may have stemmed from the need to address two gaps in his quest for the presidency, the first was that he needed to appeal to the traditional Republican Party base; the other was the need to be more likeable to Senator Hillary Clinton's supporters. The issues McCain had with his party members may have been that he acted independent of the Republican Party agenda in the Senate. He was known as some kind of Republican maverick. His call for fiscal responsibility in the face of Bush's financial profligacy created enemies for him. Probably to shore up his base, and increase his ratings in the polls, he took a gamble. He picked a candidate he had only met once. Reactions to Alaskan governor's knowledge of what was expected and her perceived level of intelligence to grasp complex issues of governance and economics, made a sham of his decision, thus casted his quest for the office of US President as farcical. Many respected conservative newspapers disgusted at her level of ignorance, openly castigated him and joyfully endorsed Obama, a notable one is the Chicago Tribune, a conservative paper that had never endorsed any liberal in its' over a century history, came out and endorsed Barack Obama with flowery statement acknowledging his brilliance, charm and unstained politics.

It sufficed to say that in other elections, crude language and nasty suggestions by Ms Palin could have upstaged the issues, created diversions, offered little in terms of solutions but could cause a viable candidate to lose. That was the hope of McCain's campaign, when the campaign manager was quoted as saying that, if they kept "discussing the issues," his candidate will lose the election. They did try to sell a dummy to the American people, but the financial and economic woes weighed too much on the minds of the people to be easily upstaged.

The maverick brand was a selling point for McCain and his Vice- Presidential nominee, they both laid claims to being independent of their party, yet they wanted the voters to vote for their party. Obama never bought the gimmick, he constantly reminded Americans that a vote for McCain was a vote for Bush, essentially a Bush third term. That infuriated the opposition. During one of the Presidential debates, McCain angrily asked Obama to look back four years for a Bush presidency; he suggested that if Obama wanted to run against Bush, he should have ran four years before. Because Obama did such a wonderful job of linking McCain's Tax cut proposal as an extension of Bush's and his insistence to stay the course in Iraq forever as Bush's blue print, the claim stuck.

The strategy employed by the Obama's campaign was to offer a new message to Americans. The people were invited to be integral part of an effort to effect change through self improvement, collective participation, and ownership of the political process. Obama's personal tactics was to remain above the fray, while he offered intelligent solutions to the issues; he stayed focused on the message. His approach was to keep calm under tense situation; he got involved only to offer solution, while others become part of the problem. The $700M bail –out created an opportunity for both presidential candidates to present a bi-partisan approach, but the chance was lost on McCain. When, he unwisely declared that he was suspending his campaign to go to Washington, creating an impression of panic, and a lack of ability on his part to multi-task. Obama on the other hand, was stunned by McCain's action; he refused to suspend his campaign. He declared that the Presidential debate should go on, and chastised his opponent for suggesting that the debate may be postponed. Obama gave the example of the lame duck President, who attended Presidential debates, while prosecuting war, he demanded his opponent multi-task.

Barack Obama refrained from joining the chorus of expediency or populism. After the Wall Street "melt down", and the whole nation was looking for answers, McCain rushed to town with his now infamous statement "The fundamentals of our economy are strong", Obama's response was delayed, but more measured. When it came, he asked for calm and demanded for hope in despair. In response to series of questionings regarding Mr. Ayers, Obama responded that he surrounded himself with people of mostly accomplished presence, intelligent friends who added value, in whom were mutual benefits. His friends were not imaginary persons of questionable character, as depicted by Governor Palin. He was also not interested in palling around with "terrorist. By campaigning on the issues, Obama was able to overcome the much vaulted Bradley effect, he made the blue collar workers see reason to place their bet on him, to hope for change and demand better treatment from their government.

Chapter 4

The Obama Message- As I see it.

His Speech

Long before the Presidential campaign of 2008, Obama called out in 2004 to all Americans at the Democratic Party convention for the nomination of John Kerry as the Party's presidential candidate. In that speech, he proposed a country where citizens closed ranks, to determine what unites, shun what divides and reduce the presence of poverty and banish hunger. He hoped for a country not cocooned by red/blue lines, or ideology, or by cultural differences, he called for a blurring of Blue states and Red states identity. He wanted to awaken the commonalities in Americans; he stated that basic needs of the citizens, whether they lived in the so called Red states (Republican stronghold), were not any different from those who lived in the Blue states (Democrats stronghold). He identified the need for social justice, equality and fair play, not as an exclusive issue between blacks, and whites or between the immigrants and the citizens, but as a need for all Americans.

His central theme was that if a Texan was not able to afford adequate medical care for his family, due to unemployment, or for the reason of inadequate health insurance provision by his employer. Then he is in no better shape than his counter part in say a blue state like Illinois, who through no fault of his was not able to afford full medical treatment for a pre-existing condition. He was concerned that when health care insurance policy is presented to the average covered person, enrollment details were not fully disclosed, and when disclosed, not fully understood. He was worried that when a card carrying member of the Republican Party began to fall behind on his mortgage payments, risking foreclosure on his home, he may not get the desired help from a broken system, any more that an Independent or even a Democrat.

He had long alerted the government, on the now obvious failed lending practice, on the need to regulate the sector. He wanted a safety net for homeowners, put in place by the government, to assist those falling behind, on their mortgages keep their homes. He approached the free market economic theory from the perspective of a risk averter, a fiscally responsible capitalist. He advocated a system where the gains flow from bottom up, as opposed to the idea that largess should trickle from top to bottom. He advocated equal days' pay for equivalent day's job for man as well as for a woman. On the issue of race, he demanded that Americans focus more on common humanity, rather than the texture of the skin.

As the electioneering heated up, I wrote this piece of open letter to Barack Obama on October 30th 2008.

My letter to the President
My Dear President -in waiting,

I would spend all I have to see true change in the politics and economics of the greatest superpower in our time, that being said for you and your campaign.

I admire your personal sense of integrity and stoic presence at all times. I know as one of my sons once said of you, that you inspire more than just hope, you inspire a true sense of belonging, friendship and love. This country and in larger sense the world needs your win come November 4th 2008.

I do solemnly wish, hope and pray that the Almighty God, the Accomplisher, grants his authority to your presidency.

Let me say quickly here that I don't want to think anyone hates you or your family, I think they despise the good message you stand for.

Keep the hope alive and perform to the best of your ability in the White House and outside of it, remember that you will be tested from all sides of the aisle, continue to find strength in the power above and the good counsel of your trusted aide, especially your wife. I do truly admire her and your daughters.

I am not an economist, but I am an entrepreneur and an inventor, my advice to your economic team as follows:

1) Keep the interest rate low for home owner generally to be able to meet their commitment

2) Work out a new credit system that favors payment based on individual disposable income

3) Establish a form of reducing balance on property mortgages, with corresponding reduced payment obligations

4) Work to reduce government investment in these huge "too big to fail banks" and eventually divest tax payers money, with intent to make good returns on such funds.

5) Encourage top corporation CEO to sacrifice their now outrageously huge pay outs for more reasonable compensation.

6) Provide incentive to hire local, invest local, and back- to-US re-sourcing (my make term sir).

7) Push for wage adjustment for middle and lower levels of the work force.

8) Don't forget our facilities, I trust you know better than I do what relief and joy these bring to all of us.

9) Lastly keep smiling. and....

10) My love to your family

I have voted for you, my wife has and we have encouraged all those we know to do the same, I may not be able to join you in the White house but I am comforted in the fact that you have excellent individuals as able experts working for the country first and your success as our president in the Oval office.

May the Lord Bless you and the rest of us all
I remain your loyal supporter

Shehu Bankole-Hameed

Editorials

I do most of my reading and catching up with the daily news and happenings world wide on the internet, however, it is interesting to note that the print media is just as popular. Some of us, who do read online, tend to browse more topics and circulate the interesting ones to our friends. I find that ideas generated by columnists or contributors do find followership in readers, and more often generate conversations, which either serve to illuminate an issue or darken the prospect of an issue.

For this purpose the people who bring news to us, tend to be trusted, disliked, and at times avoided. A reader who trust a news source, may be influenced by the courier, the opposite is true in the case of distrust. I therefore find newspaper media discourse on issue very important to convey message of change or resist it. I have come to realize that even though a lot of people claim that media endorsement, of a proposal or a candidate in an election does little to affect their audience direction, the contrary is real. The preponderance of an endorsement tended to shape readers view, ever so noticeably.

If elections were a referendum on the issues or candidates, so were the endorsements of one candidate over another. A lot has been said of the percentage of blacks that voted Obama versus that of whites; also many have indicated this occurrence to mean that blacks in general voted Barack Obama for the simple reason of resemblance. The preponderance of news media endorsement of Obama over McCain did indicate as time progressed, where the pendulum was swung, even as these media outfits were not owned by blacks. The fact was that it took a win in Iowa at the primaries by Obama for the blacks to come on his train enmasse; another fact is that blacks tend to vote Democratic Party en bloc in Presidential elections.

Some will argue that endorsements by media houses or by celebrities might not make much of an impact. The messages delivered by TV, Online and print media does influence a lot of people's decisions. I think it helps a lot to have your news delivered by persons or organizations that you trust. I want to share with you the interesting coverage in terms of endorsement for the President elect Barack Obama, by select newspapers around USA and one from UK; I have reviewed and analyzed the editorials from a personal view.

The Economist

On October 30 2008, The Economist wrote to endorse Democrat Barack Obama as the next President of the most powerful nation on earth. The Economist wanted Americans to believe that all that was at stake in the elections was a bit of gamble; it felt that the election threw up two un- tested candidates in executive terms. It argued that back in 2000 America stood tall as the undisputed Superpower, at peace with a generally admiring world. The paper went down memory lane prior to George Bush's first term in office. The Economist mentioned that George Bush inherited a budget surplus, left behind by a Democrat President Bill Clinton. And wondered aloud if one of the issues President George Bush grappled with was how to spend the surplus. I believe I have the answer; Tax-cuts to the wealthy.

I am not sure if the Republican administration thought of a better plan, other than to spend. Boy, did George Bush

spend? The paper with an international reputation as conservative mouth piece, was concerned that , the Republicans
who ran the affairs of the world most powerful and prosperous
nation, could not foretell, how their actions on management
of Wall Street would come to boil. The editors acknowledged
the uneasy feelings of deep distrust, that American voters had
going into the November 4th election. The paper in an assess-
ment of both campaigns, suggested that both Obama and Mc
Cain offered hope; I disagreed, if anything McCain was the
past, representative call to fear and divisions. However the paper conceded that Mr. Obama had a better chance of restoring
America's self confidence. It stated that the Democrat would
undoubtedly be a gamble, but a safer one.

Obama according to this paper also possessed attributes
of patience, fortitude, salesmanship and strategy. I could not
agree more, these qualities were exhibited during the primaries. I found it rather interesting that if personalities were to
determine the election, Obama should not have to lose any
sleep. Obama won on the issue of personality and understanding of issues that meant much to Americans. The paper believed that Obama's middle name Hussein would help him sell
America to the world. Even as the GOP suggested otherwise,
it seemed as if all so-called negatives thrown in Obama's way
were not so negative after all. The Economist admitted that it
would herald a different kind of America, if the son of black
Kenyan father, and white Kansan woman, were to be elected to
the highest office in the nation. His eventual election, the paper
posited would start to heal wounds of racial division that had
plagued US for decades and the complaints of the blacks about
prejudices in everyday sphere.

It noted that Obama was challenged a lot of times by the
opponent about his association with "a domestic terrorist", but
the Senator decided to take the highroad, confirmed his association with the likes of Paul Volcker, Robert Rubin and Larry
Summers, distinguished persons in their chosen field of endeavor. The paper also analyzed the caliber of advice that Barack Obama received on issues, and felt comfortable with him.
Obama's decision to meet with friends and foes alike struck a

cord that resonated with the rest of the world, seeking peace. If the Economist could cast a vote, which admittedly it couldn't, the paper would have voted Obama.

The paper was irritated by McCain's choice in Vice-Presidential running mate and with the identity of the new McCain; the editors felt would do anything to win. It suggested that the time for McCain was past. It said issue was not only with Mr. Mc Cain, or his flash of independence, or even his awkward temper. It was also the fact that Sarah Palin would be the de-facto president, with no sense of urgency, preparedness or hint of intellectual rigor to occupy the oval office. The paper submitted that it was frightening to suggest that Ms Palin would occupy the highest office of the land.

The Post Dispatch

The St Louis Post Dispatch which according to the statement made on October 12th had endorsed the couple of McCain and Obama respectively for the Presidential race, made a volte face on McCain. It wrote, "Mr. McCain, the Senior Senator from Arizona, became the incredible shrinking man. He shrank from his principled stands in favor of a humane immigration policy. He shrank from his universal condemnation of torture and his condemnation of the politics of smear." The Paper declared at one point that, "A presidency is defined less by what happens in the Oval Office than by what is done by the more than 3,000 men and women the president appoints to government office. Only 600 of them are subject to Senate approval. The rest serve at the pleasure of the President."

The paper wanted us to believe that Obama would draw unto the public service dedicated people, eager to serve and be led by an inspiring trusty leader, with notable eloquence. The paper joined the chorus of many others in endorsement of Obama's choice of running mate Joe Biden, but it described his opponent's choice as "least qualified running mate since the Swedenborgian shipbuilder Arthur Sewall ran as William Jennings Bryan's No. 2 in 1896, and added a callow and shrill partisan." The paper was quick to point out that it thought Obama was right on all the issues, preferring to judge his age as a plus, indicating that his views would not be obstructed by either cold war or the Vietnam war.

Buffalo News

Another respected US newspaper The Buffalo News came out with an editorial captioned; "Obama for President." "It advised; that voters should seize the chance to elect a transformative leader. The paper went on to state inter-alia "The only thing we have to fear, a great president once said, is fear itself. Barack Obama is not afraid."

The commentary agreed with another newspaper The Boston Globe, that Barack Obama did not want to be elected by the employment of fear, rather by the appreciation of what the issues were, and the determination to take destiny into our hands. It therefore urged its audience to submit to rational thinking rather than panic and goofy calls.

The editors said they based their judgment call, after careful evaluation of his policies on war, economy, health care, energy, environment and justice, while acknowledging his other attributes, his character, intelligence and calm. In comparison to McCain however, the paper stated that Obama wanted us to replace any sense of fear with a resolve to meet the challenges, seeking to unite a diverse people, asking for understanding not fear of each other. Even as the paper praises McCain for his years of public service and his days as POW, it was quick to point out what it sees as a change from politics of decency, often practiced by McCain before running for presidency. It noted that the tone of the campaign was all together negative, with Sarah Palin running smear campaign, devoid of reason or respect, fawning racial pains, encouraging distortions and red herrings.

While McCain shouted at the very top of his voice that Obama was a threat to the rich by offering to roll back the Bush tax cut, and to give new tax cuts for the middle class Americans, the editorial board was not convinced of McCain's rhetoric, nor was the savvy voter. The paper advised its readers that an Obama candidate was transformative. I think it was also true that McCain's candidate was transformative in nature as a chameleon, running all over the place. He pandered to all issues he thought was popular, first it was a gas- tax holiday, next it was immigration reforms, and then it was about civility. Sarah Palin's choice for the VP may have hurt Mc Cain, while Obama's selection of Joe Biden confirmed his first decision as quite thoughtful.

The following editorial has been reproduced in full with the kind permission of the respective publishers.

Seacoastonline

"The New Hampshire presidential primary gave us a unique vantage point from which to consider the attributes of the two major presidential candidates seeking our vote on Nov. 4. We saw Republican Sen. John McCain return from political exile and win through sheer force of personal will.

Democratic Sen. Barack Obama finished a close second to rival Sen. Hillary Clinton, but his concession speech last January was eloquent and defiant. "I'm still fired up and ready to go," he said. "There is something happening in the country — we are ready to take the country in a new direction."

We have no doubt about where the political direction of the country should go. It's a simple question of going backward or taking a major leap forward. When Americans cast their ballots on Nov. 4, Obama is our clear and convincing choice for president to lead the country come January.

During the lengthy campaign, Obama has unleashed a call to action for the entire country through his inspiring rhetoric and his ability to draw millions of new voters, young and old and across the political spectrum, into the ranks of those demanding an entirely new approach to governance.

We have seen the young senator from Illinois grow dramatically as a candidate and prove his leadership in the most closely contested primary process in American history. Through one of the most creative and stable political organizations ever built, he has set the bar high and insisted that Americans rise above their partisan squabbles and fears to create a government and society that will work better for the common, long-term good of the country.

While much attention has been focused on his style, Obama has methodically developed from the ground up an ambitious yet pragmatic agenda to deal with most vexing issues of our time. These include: comprehensive economic recovery, health-care reform, the need for an energy policy that will move the country away from its oil-based addiction, and restoring America's weakened reputation in the world while dealing with real threats.

No president has faced such a roster of immediate challenges since Franklin Roosevelt in 1933 during the midst of the Great Depression, and Lincoln in 1861 with the country on the verge of a civil war. Both of these elections set the country on a course of dramatic transformational change.

We believe that Obama is the leader to guide America through this tumultuous storm. Beginning last month when news of the financial crisis began to dominate the headlines, voters have had a rare opportunity to measure the leadership capabilities of Obama and McCain. While Obama remained cool and confident, McCain embodied a different policy and approach with each passing day. The less experienced Obama showed sound judgment and offered Americans a path to recovery backed by a wide range of serious policy options.

This has been a tough election. Obama has been attacked as a celebrity lightweight, a terrorist sympathizer or a latent socialist. But these attacks have had little relevance to what is needed to move this country forward after eight years of economic decay and leadership atrophy.

Obama has played tough himself, but has almost always responded on policy-based grounds. When confronted by the controversy and public concern about his former preacher earlier this year, Obama turned it into one of the great speeches on race in the country's history.

This is one of those rare elections that will truly achieve historic significance. We believe Barack Obama has shown the right temperament, judgment and intellectual vigor to be a great president — one the country needs when it matters the most."

The Seed

An endorsement from the editors of Seed; reproduced with kind permission from the publishers

"Our world is more complex, dynamic, and interdependent than at any time in recent history. Financial markets are in turmoil, geopolitical conflicts abound, and our pale blue dot is in serious peril. Yet these are also times for great optimism — about what can be known and what can be accomplished, about our potential to discover and innovate. To navigate this new reality, to realize opportunity within this massive change, we need a new approach to governance and problem solving; we need a new way of looking at the world and a new set of values founded on the conviction that knowledge is good; and we need leaders who have the courage and wisdom to change their mind in the face of new evidence. Today we stand at an inflection point in modern history, and America, still inarguably and essentially the world's beacon, will chart the way forward next Tuesday. At this critical moment, we offer an endorsement and a perspective that we hope informs the decision of our American readers.

It is abundantly evident that science can refuel economic growth, address the energy and climate challenge, and help restore America's soft power around the world. President Bush dismissed this potential, turned the very act of defying science into an art, and in so doing diminished US competitiveness and disenfranchised the country's source of innovation. His administration not only disregarded evidence time and time again but also rejected and debased the very enterprise that offered that evidence. Renewing the promise of science starts first and foremost with restoring scientific integrity to government.

Sen. Obama's pledged stance on science resonates with us. He has vowed to restore integrity to the role of science advisor by reestablishing the senior status of the Assistant to the

President for Science and Technology, and more broadly, by surrounding himself with individuals with exemplary scientific credentials; his selection of Dr. Harold Varmus as the campaign's science advisor was a very promising and laudable step in that direction. Sen. Obama understands that basic research is fundamental to how scientific advances are made. He sees the importance of expanding funding for "high-risk, high-return" work, strengthening tax policy to spur R&D, and encouraging the careers of young scientists who pursue innovative lines of thinking. He has offered a comprehensive plan to reinvigorate math and science education, and he recognizes the vital importance of re-architecting nationwide science literacy for these times. His positions on topics ranging from agriculture, alternative energy, and medical research to internet policy, patent law, and space are more robust and ultimately more in line with scientific consensus than those of Sen. McCain. These are important policy positions, and they reflect Sen. Obama's appreciation of the need to invest in science and science education as a precondition for growth and prosperity in the 21st century. We recognize, however, that these are not the issues that most voters will be thinking about when they cast their ballot.

Far more important is this: Science is a way of governing, not just something to be governed. Science offers a methodology and philosophy rooted in evidence, kept in check by persistent inquiry, and bounded by the constraints of a self-critical and rigorous method. Science is a lens through which we can and should visualize and solve complex problems, organize government and multilateral bodies, establish international alliances, inspire national pride, restore positive feelings about America around the globe, embolden democracy, and ultimately, lead the world. More than anything, what this lens offers the next administration is a limitless capacity to handle all that comes its way, no matter how complex or unanticipated.

Sen. Obama's embrace of transparency and evidence-based decision-making, his intelligence and curiosity echo this new way of looking at the world. And that is what we should be weighing in the voting booth. For his positions and, even more, for his way of coming to them, we endorse Barack Obama for President of the United States."

Chapter 5

THE General Elections

Party National Conventions- Democrats:

Senator Hillary Clinton's loss of the bid to win her party's nomination was seen by many as a let- down the leaders of the Party. Millions of her supporters cried foul, "she was treated like that because she is a woman", they wrote on her web site.

The candidate herself did not initially help matters as she did not concede easily. Super delegates from her state (New York) like Senator Charles Schumer and Governor David Paterson had to wade in, to prevail on her to give in, for the sake of the party- winning in November general elections. She had a lot to worry about; her campaign was in debt, to her and other vendors, while Obama's was awash with green backs. Eventually she came around like a good politician and offered to work for Obama's campaign for success at the polls. She moved the motion at the Party's Convention for a nomination by acclamation for Barack Obama, a unity that helped the Democratic Party in the general elections.

The Democratic National Convention was held in Denver, Colorado from August 25th through August 28th at the Pepsi center, show- casing America's moment of glory. The Democratic Party had just made history by the choice of an African-American man, the son of a black Kenyan father and White Kansan woman to bear the flag of the party in the presidential contest slated for November 2008.

The mood was joyous, ecstatic and victorious, for speakers after speakers, the Party's Vice –Presidential nominee Senator Joe Biden, President Bill Clinton and Senator Hillary Clinton, and the First Lady in-waiting Michelle Obama. Everyone was in their best, they extolled the values of democracy, and they thanked their supporters for their efforts and cash. They also called on the party to unite behind their new leader Senator Barack Obama, who was ushered in with much fanfare and happiness. Accepting the party nomination: Barack Obama spoke eloquently that night to the party supporters and Americans in general, he said;

Obama's Acceptance Speech

"Thank you, everybody, to Chairman Dean and my great friend Dick Durbin, and to all my fellow citizens of this great nation. With profound gratitude and great humility, I accept your nomination for Presidency of the United States. Let me express my thanks to the historic slate of candidates who accompanied me on this journey, and especially the one who traveled the farthest, a champion for working Americans and an inspiration to my daughters and to yours, Hillary Rodham Clinton.

To President Clinton, to President Bill Clinton, who made last night the case for change as only he can make it. To Ted Kennedy, who embodies the spirit of service, and to the next vice president of the United States, Joe Biden, I thank you.

I am grateful to finish this journey with one of the finest statesmen of our time, a man at ease with everyone from world leaders to the conductors on the Amtrak train he still takes home every night.

To the love of my life, our next first lady, Michelle Obama and to Malia and Sasha, I love you so much, and I am so proud of you.

Four years ago, I stood before you and told you my story, of the brief union between a young man from Kenya and a young woman from Kansas who weren't well-off or well-known, but shared a belief that in America their son could achieve whatever he put his mind to.

It is that promise that's always set this country apart, that through hard work and sacrifice each of us can pursue our individual dreams, but still come together as one American family, to ensure that the next generation can pursue their dreams, as well. That's why I stand here tonight. Because for 232 years, at each moment when that promise was in jeopardy, ordinary men and women -- students and soldiers, farmers and teachers, nurses and janitors -- found the courage to keep it alive.

We meet at one of those defining moments, a moment when our nation is at war, our economy is in turmoil, and the American promise has been threatened once more.

Tonight, more Americans are out of work and more are working harder for less. More of you have lost your homes and even more are watching your home values plummet. More of you have cars you can't afford to drive, credit cards, bills you can't afford to pay, and tuition that's beyond your reach.

These challenges are not all of government's making. But the failure to respond is a direct result of a broken politics in Washington and the failed policies of George W. Bush.

America, we are better than these last eight years. We are a better country than this. This country is more decent than one where a woman in Ohio, on the brink of retirement, finds herself one illness away from disaster after a lifetime of hard work.

We're a better country than one where a man in Indiana has to pack up the equipment that he's worked on for 20 years and watch as it's shipped off to China, and then chokes up as he explains how he felt like a failure when he went home to tell his family the news.

We are more compassionate than a government that lets veterans sleep on our streets and families slide into poverty that sits on its hands while a major American city drowns before our eyes.

Tonight, tonight, I say to the people of America, to Democrats and Republicans and independents across this great land: Enough. This moment, this election is our chance to keep, in the 21st century, the American promise alive.

Because next week, in Minnesota, the same party that

brought you two terms of George Bush and Dick Cheney will ask this country for a third.

And we are here -- we are here because we love this country too much to let the next four years look just like the last eight.

On November 4th, on November 4th, we must stand up and say: Eight is enough.

Now let there be no doubt. The Republican nominee, John McCain, has worn the uniform of our country with bravery and distinction, and for that we owe him our gratitude and our respect.

And next week, we'll also hear about those occasions when he's broken with his party as evidence that he can deliver the change that we need.

But the record's clear: John McCain has voted with George Bush 90 percent of the time.

Senator McCain likes to talk about judgment, but, really, what does it say about your judgment when you think George Bush has been right more than 90 percent of the time?

I don't know about you, but I am not ready to take a 10 percent chance on change.

The truth is, on issue after issue that would make a difference in your lives -- on health care, and education, and the economy -- Senator McCain has been anything but independent.

He said that our economy has made great progress under this president. He said that the fundamentals of the economy are strong.

And when one of his chief advisers, the man who wrote his economic plan, was talking about the anxieties that Americans are feeling, he said that we were just suffering from a mental recession and that we've become, and I quote, "a nation of whiners."

A nation of whiners? Tell that to the proud auto workers at a Michigan plant who, after they found out it was closing, kept showing up every day and working as hard as ever, because they knew there were people who counted on the brakes that they made.

Tell that to the military families who shoulder their burdens silently as they watch their loved ones leave for their third, or fourth, or fifth tour of duty.

These are not whiners. They work hard, and they give back, and they keep going without complaint. These are the Americans I know.

Now, I don't believe that Senator McCain doesn't care what's going on in the lives of Americans; I just think he doesn't know.

Why else would he define middle-class as someone making under $5 million a year? How else could he propose hundreds of billions in tax breaks for big corporations and oil companies, but not one penny of tax relief to more than 100 million Americans?

How else could he offer a health care plan that would actually tax people's benefits, or an education plan that would do nothing to help families pay for college, or a plan that would privatize Social Security and gamble your retirement?

It's not because John McCain doesn't care; it's because John McCain doesn't get it.

For over two decades -- for over two decades, he's subscribed to that old, discredited Republican philosophy: Give more and more to those with the most and hope that prosperity trickles down to everyone else.

In Washington, they call this the "Ownership Society," but what it really means is that you're on your own. Out of work? Tough luck, you're on your own. No health care? The market will fix it. You're on your own. Born into poverty? Pull yourself up by your own bootstraps, even if you don't have boots. You are on your own.

Well, it's time for them to own their failure. It's time for us to change America. And that's why I'm running for president of the United States.

You see, you see, we Democrats have a very different measure of what constitutes progress in this country.

We measure progress by how many people can find a job that pays the mortgage, whether you can put a little extra money away at the end of each month so you can someday watch your child receive her college diploma.

We measure progress in the 23 million new jobs that were created when Bill Clinton was president. When the average American family saw its income go up $7,500 instead of go down $2,000, like it has under George Bush.

We measure the strength of our economy not by the number of billionaires we have or the profits of the Fortune 500, but by whether someone with a good idea can take a risk and start a new business, or whether the waitress who lives on tips can take a day off and look after a sick kid without losing her job, an economy that honors the dignity of work.

The fundamentals we use to measure economic strength are whether we are living up to that fundamental promise that has made this country great, a promise that is the only reason I am standing here tonight.

Because, in the faces of those young veterans who come back from Iraq and Afghanistan, I see my grandfather, who signed up after Pearl Harbor, marched in Patton's army, and was rewarded by a grateful nation with the chance to go to college on the G.I. Bill.

In the face of that young student, who sleeps just three hours before working the night shift, I think about my mom, who raised my sister and me on her own while she worked and earned her degree, who once turned to food stamps, but was still able to send us to the best schools in the country with the help of student loans and scholarships.

When another worker tells me that his factory has shut down, I remember all those men and women on the South Side of Chicago who I stood by and fought for two decades ago after the local steel plant closed.

And when I hear a woman talk about the difficulties of starting her own business or making her way in the world, I think about my grandmother, who worked her way up from the secretarial pool to middle management, despite years of being passed over for promotions because she was a woman.

She's the one who taught me about hard work. She's the one who put off buying a new car or a new dress for herself so that I could have a better life. She poured everything she had into me. And although she can no longer travel, I know that she's watching tonight and that tonight is her night, as well.

Now, I don't know what kind of lives John McCain thinks that celebrities lead, but this has been mine.

These are my heroes; theirs are the stories that shaped my life. And it is on behalf of them that I intend to win this election and keep our promise alive as president of the United States.

What -- what is that American promise? It's a promise that says each of us has the freedom to make of our own lives what we will, but that we also have obligations to treat each other with dignity and respect.

It's a promise that says the market should reward drive and innovation and generate growth, but that businesses should live up to their responsibilities to create American jobs, to look out for American workers, and play by the rules of the road.

Ours is a promise that says government cannot solve all our problems, but what it should do is that which we cannot do for ourselves: protect us from harm and provide every child a decent education; keep our water clean and our toys safe; invest in new schools, and new roads, and science, and technology.

Our government should work for us, not against us. It should help us, not hurt us. It should ensure opportunity not just for those with the most money and influence, but for every American who's willing to work.

That's the promise of America, the idea that we are responsible for ourselves, but that we also rise or fall as one nation, the fundamental belief that I am my brother's keeper, I am my sister's keeper.

That's the promise we need to keep. That's the change we need right now.

So let me spell out exactly what that change would mean if I am president.

Change means a tax code that doesn't reward the lobbyists who wrote it, but the American workers and small businesses who deserve it.

You know, unlike John McCain, I will stop giving tax breaks to companies that ship jobs overseas, and I will start giving them to companies that create good jobs right here in America.

I'll eliminate capital gains taxes for the small businesses and start-ups that will create the high-wage, high-tech jobs of tomorrow.

I will, listen now, I will cut taxes for 95 percent of all working families, because, in an economy like this, the last thing we should do is raise taxes on the middle class.

And for the sake of our economy, our security, and the future of our planet, I will set a clear goal as president: In 10 years, we will finally end our dependence on oil from the Middle East.

We will do this. Washington -- Washington has been talking about our oil addiction for the last 30 years. And, by the way, John McCain has been there for 26 of them.

And in that time, he has said no to higher fuel-efficiency standards for cars, no to investments in renewable energy, no to renewable fuels. And today, we import triple the amount of oil than we had on the day that Senator McCain took office.

Now is the time to end this addiction and to understand that drilling is a stop-gap measure, not a long-term solution, not even close.

As president, as president, I will tap our natural gas reserves, invest in clean coal technology, and find ways to safely harness nuclear power. I'll help our auto companies re-tool, so that the fuel-efficient cars of the future are built right here in America.

I'll make it easier for the American people to afford these new cars.

And I'll invest $150 billion over the next decade in affordable, renewable sources of energy -- wind power, and solar power, and the next generation of biofuels -- an investment that will lead to new industries and 5 million new jobs that pay well and can't be outsourced.

America now is not the time for small plans. Now is the time to finally meet our moral obligation to provide every child a world-class education, because it will take nothing less to compete in the global economy.

You know, Michelle and I are only here tonight because we were given a chance at an education. And I will not settle for an America where some kids don't have that chance.

I'll invest in early childhood education. I'll recruit an army of new teachers, and pay them higher salaries, and give them more support. And in exchange, I'll ask for higher standards and more accountability.

And we will keep our promise to every young American: If you commit to serving your community or our country, we will make sure you can afford a college education.

Now is the time to finally keep the promise of affordable, accessible health care for every single American.

If you have health care -- if you have health care, my plan will lower your premiums. If you don't, you'll be able to get the same kind of coverage that members of Congress give themselves.

And as someone who watched my mother argue with insurance companies while she lay in bed dying of cancer, I will make certain those companies stop discriminating against those who are sick and need care the most.

Now is the time to help families with paid sick days and better family leave, because nobody in America should have to choose between keeping their job and caring for a sick child or an ailing parent.

Now is the time to change our bankruptcy laws, so that your pensions are protected ahead of CEO bonuses, and the time to protect Social Security for future generations.

And now is the time to keep the promise of equal pay for an equal day's work, because I want my daughters to have the exact same opportunities as your sons.

Now, many of these plans will cost money, which is why I've laid out how I'll pay for every dime: by closing corporate loopholes and tax havens that don't help America grow.

But I will also go through the federal budget line by line, eliminating programs that no longer work and making the ones we do need work better and cost less, because we cannot meet 21st-century challenges with a 20th-century bureaucracy.

And, Democrats, Democrats, we must also admit that fulfilling America's promise will require more than just money. It will require a renewed sense of responsibility from each of us to recover what John F. Kennedy called our intellectual and moral strength.

Yes, government must lead on energy independence, but each of us must do our part to make our homes and businesses more efficient.

Yes, we must provide more ladders to success for young men who fall into lives of crime and despair. But we must also admit that programs alone can't replace parents that government can't turn off the television and make a child do her homework, that fathers must take more responsibility to provide love and guidance to their children.

Individual responsibility and mutual responsibility, that's the essence of America's promise, and just as we keep our promise to the next generation here at home, so must we, keep America's promise abroad.

If John McCain wants to have a debate about who has the temperament and judgment to serve as the next commander-in-chief, that's a debate I'm ready to have.

For while Senator McCain was turning his sights to Iraq just days after 9/11, I stood up and opposed this war, knowing that it would distract us from the real threats that we face.

When John McCain said we could just muddle through in Afghanistan, I argued for more resources and more troops to finish the fight against the terrorists who actually attacked us on 9/11, and made clear that we must take out Osama bin Laden and his lieutenants if we have them in our sights.

You know, John McCain likes to say that he'll follow bin Laden to the gates of Hell, but he won't even follow him to the cave where he lives.

And today, today, as my call for a timeframe to remove our troops from Iraq has been echoed by the Iraqi government and even the Bush administration, even after we learned that Iraq has $79 billion in surplus while we are wallowing in deficit, John McCain stands alone in his stubborn refusal to end a misguided war.

That's not the judgment we need; that won't keep America safe. We need a president who can face the threats of the future, not keep grasping at the ideas of the past.

You don't defeat -- you don't defeat a terrorist network that operates in 80 countries by occupying Iraq. You don't protect Israel and deter Iran just by talking tough in Washington. You can't truly stand up for Georgia when you've strained our oldest alliances.

If John McCain wants to follow George Bush with more tough talk and bad strategy, that is his choice, but that is not the change that America needs.

We are the party of Roosevelt. We are the party of Kennedy. So don't tell me that Democrats won't defend this country. Don't tell me that Democrats won't keep us safe.

The Bush-McCain foreign policy has squandered the legacy that generations of Americans, Democrats and Republicans, have built, and we are here to restore that legacy.

As commander-in-chief, I will never hesitate to defend this nation, but I will only send our troops into harm's way with a clear mission and a sacred commitment to give them the equipment they need in battle and the care and benefits they deserve when they come home.

I will end this war in Iraq responsibly and finish the fight against Al Qaida and the Taliban in Afghanistan. I will rebuild our military to meet future conflicts, but I will also renew the tough, direct diplomacy that can prevent Iran from obtaining nuclear weapons and curb Russian aggression.

I will build new partnerships to defeat the threats of the 21st century: terrorism and nuclear proliferation, poverty and genocide, climate change and disease.

And I will restore our moral standing so that America is once again that last, best hope for all who are called to the cause of freedom, who long for lives of peace, and who yearn for a better future.

These -- these are the policies I will pursue. And in the weeks ahead, I look forward to debating them with John Mc-Cain.

But what I will not do is suggest that the senator takes his positions for political purposes, because one of the things that we have to change in our politics is the idea that people cannot disagree without challenging each other's character and each other's patriotism.

The times are too serious, the stakes are too high for this same partisan playbook. So let us agree that patriotism has no party. I love this country, and so do you, and so does John Mc-Cain.

The men and women who serve in our battlefields may be Democrats and Republicans and independents, but they have fought together, and bled together, and some died together under the same proud flag. They have not served a red America or a blue America; they have served the United States of America.

So I've got news for you, John McCain: We all put our country first.

America, our work will not be easy. The challenges we face require tough choices. And Democrats, as well as Republicans, will need to cast off the worn-out ideas and politics of the past, for part of what has been lost these past eight years can't just be measured by lost wages or bigger trade deficits. What has also been lost is our sense of common purpose, and that's what we have to restore.

We may not agree on abortion, but surely we can agree on reducing the number of unwanted pregnancies in this country.

The reality of gun ownership may be different for hunters in rural Ohio than they are for those plagued by gang violence in Cleveland, but don't tell me we can't uphold the Second Amendment while keeping AK-47s out of the hands of criminals.

I know there are differences on same-sex marriage, but surely we can agree that our gay and lesbian brothers and sisters deserve to visit the person they love in a hospital and to live lives free of discrimination.

You know, passions may fly on immigration, but I don't know anyone who benefits when a mother is separated from

her infant child or an employer undercuts American wages by
hiring illegal workers.

But this, too, is part of America's promise; the promise of a
democracy where we can find the strength and grace to bridge
divides and unite in common effort.

I know there are those who dismiss such beliefs as happy
talk. They claim that our insistence on something larger, something firmer, and more honest in our public life is just a Trojan
horse for higher taxes and the abandonment of traditional values.

And that's to be expected, because if you don't have any
fresh ideas, then you use stale tactics to scare voters.

If you don't have a record to run on, then you paint your
opponent as someone people should run from. You make a big
election about small things.

And you know what? It's worked before; because it feeds
into the cynicism we all have about government. When Washington doesn't work, all its promises seem empty. If your hopes
have been dashed again and again, then it's best to stop hoping
and settle for what you already know.

I get it. I realize that I am not the likeliest candidate for this
office. I don't fit the typical pedigree, and I haven't spent my
career in the halls of Washington.

But I stand before you tonight because all across America
something is stirring. What the naysayers don't understand is
that this election has never been about me; it's about you.

It's about you. For 18 long months, you have stood up, one
by one, and said, "Enough," to the politics of the past. You understand that, in this election, the greatest risk we can take is to
try the same, old politics with the same, old players and expect
a different result.

You have shown what history teaches us, that at defining
moments like this one; the change we need doesn't come from
Washington. Change comes to Washington.

Change happens -- change happens because the American
people demand it, because they rise up and insist on new ideas
and new leadership, a new politics for a new time.

America, this is one of those moments. I believe that, as

hard as it will be, the change we need is coming, because I've seen it, because I've lived it.

Because I've seen it in Illinois, when we provided health care to more children and moved more families from welfare to work.

I've seen it in Washington, where we worked across party lines to open up government and hold lobbyists more accountable, to give better care for our veterans, and keep nuclear weapons out of the hands of terrorists.

And I've seen it in this campaign, in the young people who voted for the first time and the young at heart; those who got involved again after a very long time; in the Republicans who never thought they'd pick up a Democratic ballot, but did.

I've seen it -- I've seen it in the workers who would rather cut their hours back a day, even though they can't afford it, than see their friends lose their jobs; in the soldiers who re-enlist after losing a limb; in the good neighbors who take a stranger in when a hurricane strikes and the floodwaters rise.

You know, this country of ours has more wealth than any nation, but that's not what makes us rich. We have the most powerful military on Earth, but that's not what makes us strong. Our universities and our culture are the envy of the world, but that's not what keeps the world coming to our shores.

Instead, it is that American spirit, that American promise, that pushes us forward even when the path is uncertain; that binds us together in spite of our differences; that makes us fix our eye not on what is seen, but what is unseen, that better place around the bend.

That promise is our greatest inheritance. It's a promise I make to my daughters when I tuck them in at night and a promise that you make to yours, a promise that has led immigrants to cross oceans and pioneers to travel west, a promise that led workers to picket lines and women to reach for the ballot.

And it is that promise that, 45 years ago today, brought Americans from every corner of this land to stand together on a Mall in Washington, before Lincoln's Memorial, and hear a young preacher from Georgia speak of his dream.

The men and women who gathered there could've heard

many things. They could've heard words of anger and discord. They could've been told to succumb to the fear and frustrations of so many dreams deferred.

But what the people heard instead -- people of every creed and color, from every walk of life -- is that, in America, our destiny is inextricably linked, that together our dreams can be one.

"We cannot walk alone," the preacher cried. "And as we walk, we must make the pledge that we shall always march ahead. We cannot turn back."

America, we cannot turn back, not with so much work to be done; not with so many children to educate, and so many veterans to care for; not with an economy to fix, and cities to rebuild, and farms to save; not with so many families to protect and so many lives to mend.

America, we cannot turn back. We cannot walk alone.

At this moment, in this election, we must pledge once more to march into the future. Let us keep that promise, that American promise, and in the words of scripture hold firmly, without wavering, to the hope that we confess.

Thank you. God bless you. And God bless the United States of America."

The Republican Flag bearer and Vice -Presidential pick

The dust hardly settled on Obama's speech and the super star status he enjoyed, when the Republican candidate Senator John McCain took the stage on September 4th.. At the party's National Convention in Minneapolis St Paul, which lasted from September 1st to September 4th, he surprised many observers with his pick for Vice- President, the Governor of Alaska Ms Sarah Palin, a pretty, little known, middle aged lady with an internal party credential of a 'maverick', a term also used to describe McCain because of his sometimes independent streak.

McCain's acceptance Speech

Most of his speech was devoted to winning the hearts of average Americans. He spoke to honor Senator Barack Obama and his team. He talked to the issues of Economy and Education, thanked President Bush for his good works, proudly presented his running mate, then went on to add" I'm going to fight for my cause every day as your President. I'm going to fight to make sure every American has every reason to thank God, as I thank Him: that I'm an American, a proud citizen of the greatest country on earth, and with hard work, strong faith and a little courage, great things are always within our reach. Fight with me. Fight with me. Fight for what's right for our country. Fight for the ideals and character of a free people. Fight for our children's future. Fight for justice and opportunity for all.

Stand up to defend our country from its enemies. Stand up for each other; for beautiful, blessed, bountiful America. Stand up, stand up, stand up and fight. Nothing is inevitable here. We're Americans, and we never give up. We never quit. We never hide from history. We make history.

Thank you, and God Bless you."

The Campaign

The new John McCain I could not relate to. How come a right leaning independent suddenly wore the coat of an average liberal? Signs of the times I guessed; since the mantra was 'change' he wanted a piece of the action, having deputized the job of holding his party base to Ms Palin, he probably felt good sounding off to the 'undecided'- a term used for many uncommitted among Independents and even party members. These undecided were the main focus of both contenders, as every poll analyzed gave the election to the candidates who could convince majority of the Independents to vote for him.

Elections or campaign coverage by CNN, CBS, ABC, CNBC, FOX and other networks included the presentation to their audiences' analytics of the game. It was fun to watch an interactive map displayed by CNN's team; every night I entertained myself with their projections and predictions. Many of the networks did give Senator Obama a chance at winning in November, more importantly, a shot at making more in roads

to the minds of many dissatisfied independents and conservatives. Barring any Bradley effect, the CNN predicted Barack
Obama would win by a wide margin.

The campaign for the November general elections started
right after the conventions when both Presidential candidates
and their Vice-Presidential nominees took shots at each other, as they delivered their convention speeches. I sensed that
many Democrats were at first baffled by the emergence of the
relatively untested Palin. Although as an Independent, I very
much doubted her credentials. When she spoke at the Convention, I noted that for whatever it was worth, she created stir
in the minds of a lot of women. Many of them just smarting
from a showdown, (Senator Hillary Clinton's loss), eighteen
million shattered glass panes were still very much around, and
could cause damages if not nurtured carefully. Many women
who voted for Senator Clinton in their millions felt let down by
Senator Barack Obama when it appeared as if she was sidelined
for Senator Joe Biden. I felt many of these women could look
favorably to another woman of substance and dedication.

Many commentaries soon after, including in the alleged
"pro-Obama" media were full of praises and eulogies for this
untested candidate from Alaska. The Conservative media
houses created unnecessary hype, this section of the media
demanded full disclosure from Barack Obama and his team.
But they were quick to suggest that a candidate who could be
a heart beat away from the Presidency not be asked any questions. Questions- how were the ordinary Americans to know
that she truly loves US, and would not seek divisions? Indeed
she spoke, and when she did, whatever she said, spoke vol-
umes of her belief, intelligence and sense of respect. Just because Sarah Palin was the Governor of one of the states, that
produces oil and gas, the Republicans began to parade her as
the most knowledgeable on oil energy matters in US. Interesting I As an energy consultant in Nigeria, before emigrating
to the US, I do know a lot more about oil and energy than
she would care to know. Yet, no one in the press seamed to be
courageous enough to challenge her and her promoters on her
credentials

However, sometime later while Sarah Palin was being interviewed by CBS's Katie Couric, she could not answer to what newspapers she read, nor was she able to state her ideas properly. Many of her erstwhile supporters were dazed. She hit back at the press a couple of days later, accusing them of bias. It was too late for her, many that were sympathetic of her positions fled.

When Ms Palin was introduced on TV, the reaction of Barack Obama and his team was as if they had fallen into a trance. They had no quick response to her introduction. His candid response later was that he was comfortable in his choice of Joe Biden as a running mate. Many pundits went to town, suggesting he should have chosen Senator Hillary Clinton, as Vice-Presidential running mate, even if he was uncomfortable with what might have been an over bearing presence of the Clintons in the White House. My gut feeling was that while Sen. Barack Obama definitely felt good about his choice, he was not prepared for the Ace in John McCain's deck of cards, which eventually turned out to be a huge joke. Ask Tina Fey of Saturday Night Live and her very many admirers who watched her satire this "energy expert".

Obama did get himself into a mild drama when he said "You can put lipstick on a pig, but it's still a pig." McCain who was never in the news before this seemed to have found his voice. He tried selling all manners of messages to his supporters. He never understood the need for change, but only mouthed it. He was happy to skirt the issues but talk of the irrelevant. It took a defiant and bold Barack to shut the opposition up, he told them "enough is enough" lets get back to what matters to the people. As it turned out, Barack team was just fine to have taken the high road, and never to have joined issues with McCain or Palin on it. American people were tired of the old ways, the economy was the most desired of all issues. As the campaign grew nastier on both sides, former President Bill Clinton was accused of not doing much to help his wife's former opponent. He had been seen on interviews; on "Larry King Live" and "The View." Exposing sentiments considered largely unhelpful to Obama's Campaign. He gradually began to

warm towards Obama, after Chris Rock the respected African
-American comedian made it clear; he thought President Clinton was ambivalent. The scenario got a lot better when Senator Hillary Clinton offered to work for Obama's success at the
Polls. She campaigned very hard for him, herself and her husband in Michigan, Ohio, Pennsylvania and Florida, where her
supporters worked tirelessly for change.

In the first week of June 2008, Obama visited Europe, and
spoke to a huge welcoming crowd. He invited everyone in Europe and the rest of the world to partner with America to develop a new approach the issue resolution. It was gravitating,
the French dropped their previous hostile note offered a warm
handshake and returned gleefully to the fold of NATO (North
Atlantic Treaty Organization). The Germans, who saw a huge
ideological gulf, were glad when a bridge of some sort was
erected between both countries. Back home, his opponent was
screaming to Americans that we are now "Georgians" in reference to the invasion of Georgia by the Russian troops. Suddenly
a little country further to the east of US barely the size of Texas
would now adopt Americans, what sense of diplomacy. This
man was whipping up cold war sentiments, his running mate
indicated that Russia her neighbor be nuked. American voters
paid close attention to both candidates as they assessed both of
them. As far as the average conservative was concerned, Mc-
Cain spoke to the base, tough talking and cowboy mentality.
However many independents and dissatisfied conservatives,
including an entire liberal base were more comfortable with
the new image of US that Obama projected.

All Obama's European tour, and the speeches he gave never
impressed John McCain. As far as he was concerned, Obama
carried on as a celebrity of some sorts, he likened Obama to
Paris Hilton. He advised Obama to debate him on Homeland
security issues. As it turned out many families were already
tired of the uncountable lies of George Bush and Dick Cheney.
They were sick of being told about "terror level", when the roof
level was being reduced on their homes per mortgage period.
The sort of discussion majority of Americans wanted was how
to keep the roof above their heads secured, while they placed

food on their tables and a ceiling on costs of drugs. Again just as in the primaries, when everyone else continued to play politics as usual. The Republican Party ignored the yearnings of average Americans for a true change, discarded the call for a new deal, which would place America once again in the forefront of international geopolitics.

By campaigning on the issues, Obama was able to overcome the much vaulted Bradley effect. He made the blue collar workers see reason to place their bet on him, to hope for change and demand better treatment from their government. Obama team repeatedly spoke to the yearnings of the people, admonished that slash and burn politics would not work, demanded to know what was wrong being an Arab or a Muslim? He also demanded that the war in Iraq be brought to a sensible end, with attention turned to the economy. I present below what I considered major issues that helped to decide the elections and how the two candidates differed.

The Economy: Barack Obama

Concerning the economy, Obama began with an Emergency Economic Plan, which was designed to jump-start the economy. He suggested middle class tax cuts, reminded everyone that the Bush administration's tax cuts favored the rich more than the middle class. He campaigned for $25 billion dollars in a State Growth Fund to prevent state and local cuts in health, education and housing assistance. Obama also felt that another $25 billion dollars should be set aside for a jobs and growth fund. This money would replenish the Highway Trust Fund and prevent cutbacks in road and bridge maintenance, thereby saving more than 1 million jobs.

Barack Obama and Joe Biden endorsed the enactment of a windfall profits tax on excessive oil company profits to give American families an immediate $1,000 emergency energy rebate to help families pay rising bills. This greatly appealed to the American public, because of the high prices they had been forced to pay at the pump. Obama may have also played on the resentment of the American public over the huge profits that oil companies have shown in the past few years; profits that came as a direct result of their charging exorbitant amounts for their products.

Barack Obama reminded Americans that President Clinton had left a surplus when he left office but that Bush had squandered it, saying that the national debt was $6 Trillion dollars when Bush took office and that it stood at $10 Trillion dollars. Obama said that he would go through the budget line by line and cut the programs that did not work. Those remaining, he would revamp so that they were much more efficient. He endorsed a credit card Bill of Rights to protect consumers, noting that a great deal of America's financial woes was tied to heavy personal credit card debt.

Obama believed that the key to a prosperous economy was a motivated workforce; a workforce that is constantly thinking about how it can improve itself, its company's products and services, and its country. One of his more popular quotes was: "You can't have a successful Wall Street without having a successful Main Street."

Many people believed that the economy was a major factor in Obama being elected president. He had strong ideas and opinions about how to get the nation back on track. He seemed to care about middle class Americans. The Bush administration favored the wealthy more than the middle class. Middle class Americans were sick of the feeling that they had been forgotten and that their plight, their needs were insignificant. In his message of change, Obama promised them hope for a better future.

The Economy: John McCain

John McCain's plan was to recoup financial bailout costs by cutting government spending. He blamed much of the economic trouble on Washington, saying that "there is too much waste and not enough accountability there". He also stated that he would cut down on earmarks and establish priorities. He admitted that government spending was out of control and suggested government to impose some fiscal discipline to revive the economy.

McCain made many generalized statements, such as, "Americans are innocent victims of Wall Street greed" and "These are tough times. We need changes. We need to keep taxes low." Though all of the above is true, McCain gave no solid plan for turning the economy around. He did suggest insurance reform to cover violent weather patterns as well as a spending freeze on everything but Defense, Veterans and Entitlements. Because of McCain's close association with President George Bush and because many of McCain's philosophies and beliefs mirrored those of President Bush, the general voting public feared that McCain would continue policies that had driven the nation of America into financial ruin. Americans felt that the nation could not endure four more years of Bush.

McCain advocated energy independence and tax cuts for all, as well as reminding the American public that he had fought excessive government spending throughout his career. He pointed out that, as a nation, we were passing on a $10 Trillion dollar debt to our young people. He also suggested that we stop sending $700 billion dollars per year to countries that don't like America. McCain felt that the government should move into the housing market and buy up most of the bad loans in order to stabilize home values. His message fell on deaf ears. Middle class Americans had heard this type of political rhetoric before and it was no longer a message they were willing to believe in. The financial meltdown in American forced the people to consider Obama's message of change and reject the tired clichés of McCain. He never hid his scant knowledge of the economy, when asked to respond to the first wave of financial meltdown on Wall Street, he replied that "fundamentals of our economy are sound". Questioned further to explain his reasoning, he offered to define fundamentals, he replied that he meant our labor (men and women) are sound, and that they are always ready to put in their very best. An aide of his, a former chief executive of HP actually threw spanner in his works, when she affirmed that he (McCain) was not fit to head a corporation. His running mate would only offer a one liner, talk about energy and her supposed overnight expertise on a subject she could probably offer nothing.

While the debate raged on in the media and on the campaign trails on what amounted to the best approach to grow the economy and keep Americans at their job, the ground was shifting in Wall Street; many banks were shivering from the disease of sub- prime loans. These loans made to home owners by get rich quick mortgage guys, were packaged by their more greedy cousins in the bigger banks and other financial institutions, to be certain almost no financial institution was immune, these were sold to, insurance firms. These loans which ordinarily should be considered stinkers in the Oscars for junks, were sold by various participating institutions as A rated securities. Due to the complex nature of these concoctions, many investors were told it was safe to bet on them, but with no way of analyzing these pieces of garbage, most bought into it, trusting their financial advisors.

Then suddenly the volcanic eruption happened on Wall Street threw out many huge banks that made up the core of the financial sector. These securities had become red hot and highly toxic, tumbling down, and washing away many investors' life savings. Lehman brothers were left to fail, Washington Mutual Bank (WAMU) the largest savings and loan to fail in US history picked for cents on the dollar, tower high Citibank came tumbling, the whole foundations of an entire economy was brittle.

That was when John McCain went on the air to say "the fundamentals of our economy are sound", Americans were stunned at his statement. This was their finances, their hard earned sweat being drained by greedy designer wearing financial advisers. Americans know when things smell really bad, and these were not signs of strong fundamentals. All his efforts to save face fell flat; he suspended his campaign, to guess what? Take a vote of yes or no, in the Senate bail out plan He wanted to postpone the Presidential debate, but Barack Obama would have none of that he demanded that the debate go on as planned.

The Presidential Debate

The first interview was won decisively by Obama; here are excerpts of the debate that took place at Oxford Mississippi on September 26th, when asked by the moderator Jim Lehrer "Gentlemen, at this very moment tonight, where do you stand on the financial recovery plan?

Obama replied" I can't think of a more important time for us to talk about the future of the country. You know, we are at a defining moment in our history. Our nation is involved in two wars, and we are going through the worst financial crisis since the Great Depression.

And although we've heard a lot about Wall Street, those of you on Main Street I think have been struggling for a while, and you recognize that this could have an impact on all sectors of the economy.

.And you're wondering, how's it going to affect me? How's it going to affect my job? How's it going to affect my house? How's it going to affect my retirement savings or my ability to send my

children to college? So we have to move swiftly, and we have to move wisely. And I've

put forward a series of proposals that make sure that we protect taxpayers as we engage in this important rescue effort.

Number one, we've got to make sure that we've got over-sight over this whole process; $700 billion, potentially, is a lot of money.

Number two, we've got to make sure that taxpayers, when they are putting their money at risk, have the possibility of getting that money back and gains, if the market -- and when the market returns.

Number three, we've got to make sure that none of that money is going to pad CEO bank accounts or to promote golden parachutes.

And, number four; we've got to make sure that we're helping homeowners, because the root problem here has to do with the foreclosures that are taking place all across the country.

Now, we also have to recognize that this is a final verdict

on eight years of failed economic policies promoted by George Bush, supported by Senator McCain, a theory that basically says that we can

shred regulations and consumer protections and give more and more to the most, and somehow prosperity will trickle down.

It hasn't worked. And I think that the fundamentals of the economy have to be measured by whether or not the middle class is getting a fair shake. That's why I'm running for president, and that's what I hope we're going to be talking about tonight."

McCain's response to the same question"... I'm feeling a little better tonight, and I'll tell you why. Because as we're here tonight in this debate, we are seeing, for the first time in a long time, Republicans and Democrats together, sitting down, trying to work out a solution to this fiscal crisis that we're in.

And have no doubt about the magnitude of this crisis. And we're not talking about failure of institutions on Wall Street. We're talking about failures on Main Street, and people who will lose their jobs, and their credits, and their homes, if we don't fix the greatest fiscal crisis, probably in -- certainly in our time, and I've been around a little while. But the point is -- the point is, we have finally seen Republicans and Democrats sitting down and negotiating together and coming up with a package.

This package has transparency in it. It has to have accountability and oversight. It has to have options for loans to failing businesses, rather than the government taking over those loans. We have to -- it has to have a package with a number of other essential elements to it.

And, yes, I went back to Washington, and I met with my Republicans in the House of Representatives. And they weren't part of the negotiations, and I understand that. And it was the House Republicans that decided that they would be part of the solution to this problem.

But I want to emphasize one point to all Americans tonight. This isn't the beginning of the end of this crisis. This is the end of the beginning, if we come out with a package that will keep these institutions stable. And we've got a lot of work to do. And we've got to create jobs.

And one of the areas, of course, is to eliminate our dependence on foreign oil.

When asked about their individual recovery plan Obama had this to say".... I think, that we have to ask ourselves is, how did we get into this situation in the first place?

Two years ago, I warned that, because of the subprime lending mess, because of the lax regulation, that we were potentially going to have a problem and tried to stop some of the abuses in mortgages that were taking place at the time. Last year, I wrote to the secretary of the Treasury to make sure that he understood the magnitude of this problem and to call on him to bring all the stakeholders together to try to deal with it.

So -- so the question, I think, that we've got to ask ourselves is, yes, we've got to solve this problem short term. And we are going to have to intervene; there's no doubt about that.

But we're also going to have to look at, how is it that we shredded so many regulations? We did not set up a 21st-century regulatory framework to deal with these problems. And that in part has to do with an economic philosophy that says that regulation is always bad."

McCain responded to the same question as he said".... Let me point out, I also warned about Fannie Mae and Freddie Mac and warned about corporate greed and excess, and CEO pay, and all that. A lot of us saw this train wreck coming.

But there's also the issue of responsibility. You've mentioned President Dwight David Eisenhower. President Eisenhower, on the night before the Normandy invasion, went into his room, and he wrote out two letters.

One of them was a letter congratulating the great members of the military and allies that had conducted and succeeded in the greatest invasion in history, still to this day, and forever.

And he wrote out another letter, and that was a letter of resignation from the United States Army for the failure of the landings at Normandy.

Somehow we've lost that accountability. I've been heavily criticized because I called for the resignation of the chairman of the Securities and Exchange Commission. We've got to start also holding people accountable, and we've got to reward people who succeed.

But somehow in Washington today -- and I'm afraid on Wall Street -- greed is rewarded, excess is rewarded, and corruption – or certainly failure to carry out our responsibility is rewarded.

As President of the United States, people are going to be held accountable in my administration. And I promise you that that will happen."

The second Presidential debate conducted was also decided in Obama's favor, never mind, that at a point during the debate McCain referring to Barack Obama as "that one", an obviously irritated old man, trying to scold an errant young boy.

The third Presidential debate was very feisty; both men were forced to confront each other. That was not the case in the previous two debates. Senator McCain sought to irritate Senator Obama with his reference to Barack's answer to a questioned posed to him on one of his campaign stops in Ohio. When asked about how his tax plan would change, materially for folks earning above $250,000, Senator Obama explained as he was wont to at every stop, but he seemed not to have been understood. Senator McCain tried to create a big deal of the simple situation, the Obama –Biden tax plan was explained on their web site. The night ended with Obama thrashing McCain and thus setting the stage for a landslide win in November. No amount of story telling about any average Joe Six Packs, not even silly questions about Obama from McCain's supporters could derail the movement.

McCain's very caustic charge of socialist (in reference to Obama's tax plan)did not stick, as the voters were a lot smarter, they just could not buy into his fear tactics. And all hopes that introduction of Sarah Palin to energize the base and rev up the negative rhetoric, back fired, she was easily dismissed by the majority of news media as unacceptable to occupy the highest office of the land, it was obvious people did not want a repeat of Bush Cheney era. As with all rushed decisions, devoid of reasonable analysis, McCain's camp started to experience fatigue, squabbles and mutual distrust among itself, similar to what happened within the camp of Clinton's, when she had to fire a couple of aides. Only this time the rigor was a split in camps, McCain's vs. Palin's, creating tension between erstwhile partners.

McCain's team began to lose focus in the last few weeks before the election, he skipped on a pre-arranged visit to David Letterman show, he claimed he had to be in DC, and therefore could not spare time for a few humor. But he was spotted a few blocks from set of Letterman's preparing for an interview with Katie Couric; he was the butt of jokes for a while after. Sarah Palin on the other hand was sequestered from the 'hostile' press, after flunking her interview, her media presence was more of a negative pull on the campaign. Joe Biden had his own "rhetorical flourishes" as characterized by Obama, after his gaffe about Obama being tested within six months of his presidency.

Both camps began to prepare for the transition, but noticeable with a grand plan for both transition and election night party was Obama's. He got Mayor Daley of Chicago to work non stop, to provide a secure, yet open Grand Park party for him. Everyone was concerned about logistics and security implications, not Barack's team if they were bothered, they did not show it, "we leave security issues to the police and others in-charge of it" was always their response. Republicans accused Obama's camp as being too assuming, planning a transition team as if they had won, his team would reply that it was just following standard procedure mandated by policy. On the other hand, even while he trailed Obama in almost all of the so called battleground states, and with majority of the demographics, including the ever so sought after independents. McCain acted as if these mattered not, he introduced his wife as "the next first lady", only a couple of days to the elections. The wait ended on November 4th 2008, every state went to the polls, it was very peaceful, in places where rain fell, they waited patiently although wet, to get their hands on the ballot papers.

The Polls

As the polls closed in the east coast, results started to trickle in, Obama had won New Hampshire, a good sign many said, and next he took New York, Pennsylvania, the contested state of Ohio and Indiana. Hope was already very thin on the opposition camp, with Nevada, New Mexico and Florida in his favor. It appeared to me that ABC network was the first to call the day for President Obama as soon as the polls closed in California.

Grand Park immediately became a place of joy, with people of diverse belongings clinging to each other, in total amazement of the day. Captured in the crowd were many natives of Chicago, Rev. Jesse Jackson, Oprah Winfrey and many other known faces. The time has come; change indeed came to US landscape. We have a lot of people to thank for it, the restless students who volunteered to make change happen, the many who gave to the campaigns, many hip pop stars, notably Jay Z, Hollywood Stars and countless others. The courage of Obama and his family, the campaign teams of both party, Michelle Obama and her wonderful daughters Malia and Sasha, the watchful media and the very stupid policy of George Bush, that paved way for pain in the land, and hopelessness in the horizon. All above all I thank GOD.

Walking gracefully on to the podium with his wife, the incoming First Lady, Michelle Obama, his daughters Malia and Sasha, the Vice –President elect Joe Biden, his wife Jill Biden, and other members of his family, President –elect Barack Hussein Obama reminded us all of what is possible, as he spoke;

Presidential Acceptance Speech

"If there is anyone out there who still doubts that America is a place where all things are possible; who still wonders if the dream of our founders is alive in our time; who still questions the power of our democracy, tonight is your answer.

It's the answer told by lines that stretched around schools and churches in numbers this nation has never seen; by people who waited three hours and four hours, many for the very first time in their lives, because they believed that this time must be different; that their voice could be that difference.

It's the answer spoken by young and old, rich and poor, Democrat and Republican, black, white, Hispanic, Asian, Native American, gay, straight, disabled and not disabled - Americans who sent a message to the world that we have never been a collection of Red States and Blue States: we are, and always will be, the United States of America.

It's the answer that led those who have been told for so long by so many to be cynical, and fearful, and doubtful of what we can achieve to put their hands on the arc of history and bend it once more toward the hope of a better day.

It's been a long time coming, but tonight, because of what we did on this day, in this election, at this defining moment, change has come to America.

I just received a very gracious call from Senator McCain. He fought long and hard in this campaign, and he's fought even longer and harder for the country he loves. He has endured sacrifices for America that most of us cannot begin to imagine, and we are better off for the service rendered by this brave and selfless leader. I congratulate him and Governor Palin for all they have achieved, and I look forward to working with them to renew this nation's promise in the months ahead.

I want to thank my partner in this journey, a man who campaigned from his heart and spoke for the men and women he grew up with on the streets of Scranton and rode with on that train home to Delaware, the Vice President-elect of the United States, Joe Biden.

I would not be standing here tonight without the unyielding support of my best friend for the last sixteen years, the rock of our family and the love of my life, our nation's next First Lady, Michelle Obama. Sasha and Malia, I love you both so much, and you have earned the new puppy that's coming with us to the White House. And while she's no longer with us, I know my grandmother is watching, along with the family that made me who I am. I miss them tonight, and know that my debt to them is beyond measure.

To my campaign manager David Plouffe, my chief strategist David Axelrod, and the best campaign team ever assembled in the history of politics - you made this happen, and I am forever grateful for what you've sacrificed to get it done.

But above all, I will never forget who this victory truly belongs to - it belongs to you.

I was never the likeliest candidate for this office. We didn't start with much money or many endorsements. Our campaign was not hatched in the halls of Washington - it began in the back-yards of Des Moines and the living rooms of Concord and the front porches of Charleston.

It was built by working men and women who dug into what little savings they had to give five dollars and ten dollars and twenty dollars to this cause. It grew strength from the young people who rejected the myth of their generation's apathy; who left their homes and their families for jobs that offered little pay and less sleep; from the not-so-young people who braved the bitter cold and scorching heat to knock on the doors of perfect strangers; from the millions of Americans who volunteered, and organized, and proved that more than two centuries later, a government of the people, by the people and for the people has not perished from this Earth. This is your victory.

I know you didn't do this just to win an election and I know you didn't do it for me. You did it because you understand the enormity of the task that lies ahead. For even as we celebrate tonight, we know the challenges that tomorrow will bring are the greatest of our lifetime - two wars, a planet in peril, the worst financial crisis in a century. Even as we stand here tonight, we know there are brave Americans waking up in the deserts of Iraq and the mountains of Afghanistan to risk their lives for us. There are mothers and fathers who will lie awake after their children fall asleep and wonder how they'll make the mortgage, or pay their doctor's bills, or save enough for college. There is new energy to harness and new jobs to be created; new schools to build and threats to meet and alliances to repair.

The road ahead will be long. Our climb will be steep. We may not get there in one year or even one term, but America - I have never been more hopeful than I am tonight that we will get there. I promise you - we as a people will get there.

There will be setbacks and false starts. There are many who won't agree with every decision or policy I make as President, and we know that government can't solve every problem. But I will always be honest with you about the challenges we face. I will listen to you, especially when we disagree. And above all, I will ask you join in the work of remaking this nation the only way it's been done in America for two-hundred and twenty-one years - block by block, brick by brick, calloused hand by calloused hand.

What began twenty-one months ago in the depths of winter must not end on this autumn night. This victory alone is not the change we seek - it is only the chance for us to make that change. And that cannot happen if we go back to the way things were. It cannot happen without you.

So let us summon a new spirit of patriotism; of service and responsibility where each of us resolves to pitch in and work harder and look after not only ourselves, but each other. Let us remember that if this financial crisis taught us anything, it's that we cannot have a thriving Wall Street while Main Street suffers - in this country, we rise or fall as one nation; as one people.

Let us resist the temptation to fall back on the same partisanship and pettiness and immaturity that have poisoned our politics for so long. Let us remember that it was a man from this state who first carried the banner of the Republican Party to the White House - a party founded on the values of self-reliance, individual liberty, and national unity. Those are values we all share, and while the Democratic Party has won a great victory tonight, we do so with a measure of humility and determination to heal the divides that have held back our progress. As Lincoln said to a nation far more divided than ours, "We are not enemies, but friends...though passion may have strained it must not break our bonds of affection." And to those Americans whose support I have yet to earn - I may not have won your vote, but I hear your voices, I need your help, and I will be your President too.

And to all those watching tonight from beyond our shores, from parliaments and palaces to those who are huddled around radios in the forgotten corners of our world - our stories are singular, but our destiny is shared, and a new dawn of American leadership is at hand. To those who would tear this world down - we will defeat you. To those who seek peace and security - we support you. And to all those who have wondered if America's beacon still burns as bright - tonight we proved once more that the true strength of our nation comes not from our the might of our arms or the scale of our wealth, but from the enduring power of our ideals: democracy, liberty, opportunity, and unyielding hope.

For that is the true genius of America - that America can change? Our union can be perfected. And what we have already achieved gives us hope for what we can and must achieve tomorrow.

This election had many firsts and many stories that will be told for generations. But one that's on my mind tonight is about a woman who cast her ballot in Atlanta. She's a lot like the millions of others who stood in line to make their voice heard in this election except for one thing - Ann Nixon Cooper is 106 years old.

She was born just a generation past slavery; a time when there were no cars on the road or planes in the sky; when someone like her couldn't vote for two reasons - because she was a woman and because of the color of her skin.

And tonight, I think about all that she's seen throughout her century in America - the heartache and the hope; the struggle and the progress; the times we were told that we can't, and the people who pressed on with that American creed: Yes we can.

At a time when women's voices were silenced and their hopes dismissed, she lived to see them stand up and speak out and reach for the ballot. Yes we can.

When there was despair in the dust bowl and depression across the land, she saw a nation conquer fear itself with a New Deal, new jobs and a new sense of common purpose. Yes we can.

When the bombs fell on our harbor and tyranny threatened the world, she was there to witness a generation rise to greatness and a democracy was saved. Yes we can.

She was there for the buses in Montgomery, the hoses in Birmingham, a bridge in Selma, and a preacher from Atlanta who told a people that "We Shall Overcome." Yes we can.

A man touched down on the moon, a wall came down in Berlin, a world was connected by our own science and imagination. And this year, in this election, she touched her finger to a screen, and cast her vote, because after 106 years in America, through the best of times and the darkest of hours, she knows how America can change. Yes we can.

America, we have come so far. We have seen so much. But there is so much more to do. So tonight, let us ask ourselves - if our children should live to see the next century; if my daughters should be so lucky to live as long as Ann Nixon Cooper, what change will they see? What progress will we have made?

This is our chance to answer that call. This is our moment. This is our time - to put our people back to work and open doors of opportunity for our kids; to restore prosperity and promote the cause of peace; to reclaim the American Dream and reaffirm that fundamental truth - that out of many, we are one; that while we breathe, we hope, and where we are met with cynicism, and doubt, and those who tell us that we can't, we will respond with that timeless creed that sums up the spirit of a people:

Yes We Can. Thank you, God bless you, and may God Bless the United States of America."

There is hope in the land, including a state which he did not win, the state of Louisiana, where the blacks of New Orleans seemed to have been forgotten. How else does one explain that in this town, you will find black residents ushering you into a restaurant, but they are never really allowed to be waiters to earn tips and make a decent living. If anything they too can hope that finally they may also dream and "Yes they can."

Chapter 6

The Decision

With the 2008 presidential elections over, Americans are keep-ing a close eye on newly elected president, Barack Obama. He took over the largest, most powerful nation on the planet at what is possibly the worst moment in its 233-year history. Among the many challenges facing Mr. Obama are: An eco-nomic crisis that rivals the Great Depression of 1929; a seem-ingly unending war in Iraq and Afghanistan

A health care crisis affecting over 45 million Americans, growing concerns over global warming and climate change.

As if that were not enough, he took office on January 20, 2009 as our very first black President. In spite of the huge strides made by Americans in the past 30 years regarding racial prejudice, there still remains a segment of the population who silently harbor thoughts of bigotry toward black Americans. Of course, no President has ever had the full support of his constituents or the entire populace. One of the major factors in Barack Obama's successful run for the White House was the economic crisis currently raging in the US. Most Americans, in spite of political leanings, felt that none of us could afford four more years of Bush politics and if Senator McCain had been elected, most felt that that was exactly what we'd be fac-ing. Four more years of the same policies that had brought us to this very moment, a time of global economic fear such as the world had not experienced in modern history. The messages and beliefs of the two men running for President of the United

States could not have been more different. They were and are as diverse as the gulf of ideals separating both candidates.

Senator Obama ran a grassroots campaign, combining the power of a community organizer with that of a savvy internet user, to appeal to the average Joe. His message of change rang true to millions of Americans and it came at a time when Americans had all but lost hope that things could improve; that we might actually have a shot at coming through the many crises that face our nation even now.

The message of Senator McCain felt like the same old political rhetoric that most of us had become accustomed to; fear tactics, divisive and inciting speeches. Senator McCain's voice sounded like so much of the same stale political brouhaha that most Americans have come to abhor. His choice of a Vice -Presidential candidate, Sarah Palin seem to have upset a lot of Americans, it appeared to many across the isle that Ms Palin was in the least prepared to be President in waiting. She was not considered savvy enough to attend to many intelligent decisions that would be required of her, her responses to media interview, particularly with Katie Couric of CBS News was sub par. Interestingly, Obama's choice in Senator Biden was applauded by many across the isle. We were ready for that change that Barack Obama was promising. His ideas were fresh and innovative and made us believe that change was possible.

For instance, on the subject of the economy, Barack Obama, in his 43-page document titled, "Blueprint for Change", addresses in ordinary language each specific area of our economic woes and outlines exactly what he and Joe Biden, his running mate, would do to "fix" those areas. Obama doesn't just make general statements about how he will restore the economy; he addresses specific items point by point and gives us his plan to improve that area.

Elected: Barack Obama- Another look

Barack Obama was born in Honolulu, Hawaii but left the country for Indonesia with his mother and her new husband, after she divorced his father. He would return in 1971 to Hawaii to live with his maternal grandparents. There he attended a college preparatory school until his graduation from high school in 1979. He said that as a young adult he struggled with strong feelings concerning his multi-racial heritage, but believes that growing up in Hawaii where there were many cultures aided his understanding and ultimately became an integral part of his world-view.

Obama's run for presidency of the United States came at an opportune time in US history. His forthright approach to the serious issues that have taken the life out of the US economy proved to be enough, in spite of many challenges from respected candidates and seasoned politicians. He was viewed as an underdog, but after the hard fought primaries and the general election, Barack Obama has now emerged as an historic figure, the first African American to become president of the United States of America.

As historians look back at these extraordinary events, they may find a variety of reasons for this. Of the most significant, though, will certainly be the state of the economy. Americans had grown weary of Republican gospel of tax cuts; many have come to identify with Obama in his quest to relate such tax cuts to appeasing the rich while mocking the poor. Respondents to questions on who they would trust with the economy answered Democrats in huge numbers, certainly over 57% of respondents felt comfortable with the Democrats; it was obvious that such would very likely translate to an Obama victory. With companies all over the US suffering financial woes, some of them fatal, the American voting public decided to take a chance on this rookie from Illinois, praying that the hope and answers he offered would pan out.

A hard look at the academic and professional credentials of Barack Obama paint a portrait of a young man with dreams and visions and the determination to accomplish the goals he set for himself. His willingness to work hard and think outside the box makes us believe that the US has a reason to hope. Obama came to national media attention in 1991 when he became the first black president of the Harvard Law Review. His impressive career includes three years as director of the Developing Communities Project in Chicago where the annual budget went from $70,000 to $400,000 while he was director. There he helped set up a job training program and a tenant's rights organization. His career and accomplishments also paint a portrait of a man who cares about people; a man who is concerned for those less fortunate; a man who deeply loves his family and his country.

I do hope that in time, his ideas and programs can actually turn the US economy around. But when we consider the incredible achievements of another black person, Oprah Winfrey, we have reason to hope. As we consider the alternatives, hope is not a bad way to go. History will certainly credit another black man Martin Luther King Jr. with changing the political landscape of the US. Perhaps the dreams of Martin Luther King Jr. were at last realized on January 20, 2009, when Barack Obama took office as the first African American President of the United States of America.

Not Elected: John McCain

McCain was born in 1936 at a Coco Solo Naval Air Station in the Panama Canal. Both his father and grandfather were four-star admirals in the US Navy. In 1951, his family settled in Virginia and he attended an Episcopal High School where he excelled in wrestling. He graduated in 1954. After high school, he followed in the footsteps of his father and grandfather and entered the United States Naval Academy in Annapolis. Despite a high IQ, he struggled with obeying the rules and did poorly in all but his favorite subjects, literature and history.

He trained at Pensacola to become a naval aviator, completing flight school in 1960. As a young pilot, he was regarded as a risk-taker and had several accidents but no serious injuries. In 1967, while flying his 23rd bombing mission over North Vietnam, his plane was shot down by a missile over Hanoi. He fractured both legs ejecting from the airplane and nearly drowned when he parachuted into a lake. Although he was badly wounded, his captors, the North Vietnamese refused to allow him medical treatment and he is not able even today to raise his arms above his head due to those injuries. When it was discovered that his father was a top admiral, the story of his imprisonment made all the newspapers. He was released on March 14, 1973 and became a celebrity of sorts as a returning POW. He entered politics in 1977 as the Navy's liaison to the Senate. In spite of lingering physical maladies from his POW experience, McCain has led a fairly vigorous and healthy life. In 1990, it was discovered that he had skin cancer and eventually 4 malignant melanomas were removed. Since then, he has undergone periodic examinations by doctors. In August 2001, McCain noticed blood in his urine. Doctors found stones in his bladder and lasers were used to break these apart. At the same time, they surgically removed enlarged prostate tissue, which was the cause of the bleeding.

When he ran for president in 2000, as well as 2008, McCain released his medical records to the public in an effort to starve off rumors that he was incompetent for the job of president of the United States based on physical illness. Prior to the 2008 election, his doctors gave him a clean bill of health, saying that they saw no reason why he would not be able to handle the rigorous duties that go along with being president. There was considerable speculation during his campaign on the part of media and voters concerning McCain's health. Many wondered whether the youthful, inexperienced and poorly prepared Sarah Palin, could adequately perform all the duties involved in the role of the president in the event that McCain was unable to complete his term. Even more damaging though, was his friendship with George W. Bush. McCain spent much of the political race for president struggling to free himself from the doubts and suspicions of US voters concerning whether or not he would follow Bush policies should he become president.

Though McCain was a well-respected Senator from Arizona, as well as war hero, his inability to garner the necessary votes to become President may have come as a result of a combination of his ill advice choice of vice presidential candidate, and a legacy of failure by the Bush administration. In the last two years of his presidency, Bush's popularity plummeted along with the Dow Jones. He was seen as a president who was a friend of the rich man and big oil. Though a strong family man, Bush has never been viewed by the American public as a man who cared for the poor, underprivileged, and uneducated, preferring the company of the "good ole boys" he grew up with instead. McCain has always held strong views and opinions on foreign affairs. His stance on other issues such as developing "green" jobs and promoting alternative fuel sources has been lacking though. During the campaign, McCain answered many of the questions posed to him in general terms with no clear plan to solve specific dilemmas. Obama, on the other hand, laid out clear solutions to a variety of crises facing US.

Whether Obama's solutions work or not, Americans needed to hear those well-defined answers concerning subjects like, the Economic Bailout, developing "green" energy sources and the War in Iraq. McCain was unable to answer those and other critical questions with the necessary confidence to convince American voters that he was the man for the job.

Chapter 7

Other Issues and Platforms

The Housing Crisis: Barack Obama

On the subject of housing, Obama began by talking about some ways to repair the breeches in our current housing industry if future crises were to be averted. This seemed like a logical approach. He named one of the major malfunctions as mortgage fraud. Obama cited the need for stronger oversight of the mortgage lending market. He stated that government has allowed the special interest groups to set the regulatory agenda and that it is time to reconsider how we oversee financial markets. In plain English, lenders simply allowed those who were not financially able to purchase a home, to go ahead and do it anyway. In many cases, lenders would sell a $300,000 house to a family who could only afford a $150,000 house. Families were already behind 3 or 4 payments by the time they realized this and the home would go into foreclosure.

In "Blueprint for Change", Obama went on to say that he and Joe Biden would provide tax cuts of $500 for 10 million homeowners, those who earn less than $50,000 per year. This tax cut would provide direct relief to homeowners who are struggling to pay their mortgage payments. Obama believed that the current home mortgage crisis is interconnected to the nation's financial crisis. He stated that often the foreclosure of someone's home began with the homeowner losing his or her job. He believes that in order to solve one dilemma, it is necessary to address them both. He has also endorsed a proposal to fund a second "Economic Stimulus Package". Of the suggested $30 billion dollars for this economic stimulus package, he would earmark $10 billion dollars that would go toward a Foreclosure Prevention Fund. These funds would not only help families struggling to save their homes but it would also address issues of poor or faulty lending practices. Portions of the funds might also go towards counseling potential homebuyers in the area of the true cost of home ownership in order to prevent buyers from purchasing homes they are unable to afford. The Foreclosure Prevention Fund would also waive certain state and local income taxes that result from an individual selling their home to avoid foreclosure. The Fund would not help speculators, people who bought vacation homes or people who falsely represented their incomes.

The Housing Crisis: John McCain

Obama offered this on McCain "if you do not know how many houses you own, then you cannot possibly identify with the problems of foreclosure", on the other hand, McCain stated that he would stabilize the mortgage industry so that people could stay in their homes. This is a fairly general statement, which does not outline any type of plan for accomplishing his goal. He did state that he would spend $300 billion to buy up home mortgages. He also stated that we might have to go further to fix the subprime lending situation but did not have a viable solution for that problem. McCain made what he claimed was a new proposal to rescue over-mortgaged homeowners, saying "I would order the secretary of the treasury to immediately buy up the bad home loan mortgages in America and renegotiate at the diminished value of those homes and let people stay in their homes. It's my proposal. It's not Senator Obama's proposal; it's not President Bush's proposal." But, in fact, the recently passed $700 billion rescue package already granted the treasury secretary authority to undertake just such a program. It required the secretary to buy up troubled mortgages while considering "the need to help families keep their homes & to stabilize communities." It also says, "The Secretary shall consent to term extensions, rate reductions and principal write downs."

Obama himself had urged this as the package was being considered. He said, "We should consider giving the government the authority to purchase mortgages directly instead of simply purchasing mortgage-backed securities."

In 2008, McCain told local business leaders in Los Angeles that he would "consider any and all proposals based on their cost and benefits." In other statements, McCain has said that the government should not reward banks and borrowers who behave irresponsibly. He supports the balanced budget amendment.

The War: Barack Obama

Concerning the war, Obama said that we needed a new strategy. He pointed out that the war in Iraq has lasted longer than World War I, World War II or the Civil War. More than 4,000 Americans have died and a great many more have been wounded. He reminded us that US has spent $2.7 trillion dollars on the war in Iraq and its aftermath. He also believes that the war in Iraq has distracted us from capturing Bin Laden, who is a formidable threat to the American way of life. In January 2008, he stated that the war distracted us from other global threats and was conceptually flawed from the beginning. He believes that Al-Qaeda is stronger now than before the war began. He categorized the Bush/McCain strategy on war as "Tough talk and bad strategy." He went on record saying that although American soldiers have done an outstanding job in the Middle East, Iraq is a long way from being able to exist without American Military intervention. He endorsed a phased withdrawal from Iraq and a stronger effort toward forcing the Iraqi government to fund its own rebuilding. Obama believes that it is wrong for US to continue to coddle the Iraqi government and that we must insist that they move toward autonomous subsistence.

During the course of the first presidential debate, Obama made his stance on the war very clear. "I think the first question is whether we should have gone into the war in the first place. Six years ago, I opposed this war because I said that not only did we not know how much it was going to cost, what our exit strategy might be, how it would affect our relationships around the world, and whether our intelligence was sound, but also because we hadn't caught bin Laden. We hadn't put al Qaeda to rest, and as a consequence, I thought that it was going to be a distraction. I wish I had been wrong. We've spent over $600 billion so far. We have lost over 4,000 lives. We have seen 30,000 wounded, and al Qaeda is stronger now than at any time since 2001. We are still spending $10 billion a month at a time when we are in great distress here at home. The lesson is we should never hesitate to use military force, and I will not, as president, in order to keep the American people safe. But we have to use our military wisely. We did not use our military wisely in Iraq." His views and opinions mostly reflected those of the US voter.

The War: John McCain

McCain's strategy was far less detailed. He simply said that we should, "support the surge and bring troops home with honor." He did not have a detailed plan to do this. He has also made generalized statements such as, "Creating a timetable for withdrawal is a white flag of surrender", and that the way to win is to defeat al-Qaeda and limit Iran's influence. McCain admitted that the war in Iraq had not gone well and the situation there was dire but not hopeless. He said that Al Qaeda might take over the Iraqi oil wells. He made the statement that if we left Iraq, the terrorists would follow us home. McCain has said that he believes we are winning the war in Iraq, and that there is social and economic progress. He claims that the strategy of going into any area, clearing and holding it, causes the locals to come forward wishing to befriend American troops. Once this alliance takes place, the local people will inform on the terrorists and help American troops as they are able. He believes that this is a sound strategy for making progress in the Iraq war.

In his efforts to support the Bush administration's War on Terror, McCain allowed himself to be seen in a very unpopular light. In a New York Times Poll, only 5% of Americans said they trusted Bush to resolve the war in Iraq successfully. Henceforth, Americans reasoned that McCain would also not be effective in resolving the war and bringing home our troops.

Jobs: Barack Obama

Obama outlined a fairly industrious plan to create new jobs, placing emphasis on creating "green" jobs. In his document, "Blueprint for Change", he would create an "Advanced Manufacturing Fund" which would identify and invest in innovative manufacturing strategies. The Fund would have a peer-review selection and award process based on the Michigan 21st Century Jobs Fund, a state-level program that has awarded $125 million to businesses with the most ingenious suggestions to create new products and new jobs. Barack Obama and Joe Biden would also invest $150 billion over a 10-year period to advance the next generation fuel infrastructure, as well as biofuels. He suggested further commercializing of plug-in hybrids. He would promote development of renewable energy and invest in low emissions coal plants. This could begin transition to a new digital electricity grid. One of the main focuses of Barack Obama's plan would be to ensure that innovative technologies are developed in the U.S. as quickly as possible and commercialized around the world. This plan not only creates jobs, but aids with the energy crisis and the Climate Change crisis.

Many of Obama's strategies are designed to solve several dilemmas at the same time. For instance, his proposal to create new job training programs is aimed at "Green Technologies". It increases funding for federal workforce training programs and incorporates green technologies training. He would also create an energy-focused youth jobs program to invest in young people from disadvantaged homes. In this manner, the most good is accomplished with the least amount of money, time and effort. His innovative ideas and creative strategies were a pleasant surprise to most voting Americans, who had long ago given up on believing that a politician could come up with anything original.

Jobs: John McCain

On the subject of jobs for Americans, McCain suggested cutting taxes on businesses so that they wouldn't be tempted to outsource their positions to other countries. At 35%, US has the second highest business tax in the world, which is largely responsible for American businesses choosing to outsource or moving their companies outright to other nations where the business tax is lower. He also suggested overhauling unemployment as a retraining program. In September of 2008, he stated that America should "help workers find new jobs that won't go away" but did not have a viable plan to implement such a program. He voted YES on increasing the minimum wage in February of 2007, however, in the past he had voted against raising the minimum wage 19 times. McCain endorsed reducing inheritance taxes and was against the ethanol subsidy, saying that it was a waste of time and money and not worth it to the American people to pursue as an alternate fuel source. Over the years, McCain's voting record shows him to be anti-union and he has stated in the past that unions are a monopoly and workers should not be compelled to join them.

McCain believes that America should end the sugar subsidy, saying that the sugar program has resulted in US consumers paying three times the current world price for sugar. Defenders of the sugar program claim that it is critical to the viability of our domestic sugar industry. Closer examination of this program reveals that the only benefits of it are to big sugar tycoons. In a press release, McCain stated that, "Only by political clout has this corporate welfare program survived. I believe we should end the subsidies to the sugar industry and eliminate the sugar program that is unfair to consumers."

Tax Relief: Barack Obama

In his 43-page document, "Blueprint for Change", Obama and Biden outlined some of the most innovative tax reform to come down the pike in 50 years. They endorse tax cuts for working families, suggesting a $500 per year tax cut for individual workers or $1000 for each family. He has recommended an overhaul of the tax code, suggesting that it's unfair and complicated. His "Making Work Pay" tax cut would completely eliminate income taxes for 10 million Americans.   Obama would create an American Opportunity Tax Credit, which makes college affordable. This would provide $4000 per year for college education and cover two-thirds of the cost of tuition for the average university. Recipients of this tax credit would be required to conduct 100 hours of community service per year. Obama and Biden endorse reformation of the Child and Dependent Care Tax Credit. They want to make it refundable and allow low-income families to receive up to a 50 percent credit for their childcare expenses. Coupled with the "Making Work Pay" tax cut, this proposal would place more money back into the hands of hardworking low and middle-income families.

Another revolutionary change suggested by Obama was to simplify the way Americans currently file their taxes. The process would be streamlined so that millions of Americans would be able to do their taxes in about five minutes. This would greatly decrease the amount of time and money Americans spend doing their taxes each year. Obama suggested a tax cut for seniors who earn less than $50,000 per year and even proposed eliminating the need for many older Americans to file taxes at all. This would result in a savings not only of tax money but also money spent on tax preparers by senior Americans. Most Americans were surprised and delighted by all of Obama's ideas for overhauling the tax system in America. According to a 2006 Gallup Poll, over 50% of Americans feel that they pay too much in federal income taxes and those corporations and upper class citizens pay too little. Ms Palin would task Obama on his tax plan in a very negative and absurd manner, she suggested that he was introducing a system of robbing Peter to pay Paul, an obvious reference to socialism, a term she used during the last days of the campaign at many of her rallies. She tried to paint his rolling back the Bush tax cut to Clinton's era as an effort to reward lazy section of the populace against hard working class section of the populace, but all her efforts were rebuffed by the voters in large numbers.

Tax Relief: John McCain

McCain was quoted many times during the presidential race saying that taxes should not be raised during an economic downturn. He clearly stated that he would veto any tax increase, saying that it is "the worst thing you can do during shaky economic times." In other interviews, McCain has said that he believes the tax code is fair and that the wealthy pay the bulk of taxes. Statements such as this have not been well received by the voting public since middle-class Americans have long held that they shoulder the bulk of the tax burden. He did, however, endorse a $7000 per child tax exemption and the doubling of the personal tax exemption for every dependent. In August of 2008, McCain was quoted as saying, "Let's give every family in America a $7,000 tax credit for every child they have." Later his statement had to be corrected. What he meant to say was that he was in favor of a $7,000 tax exemption, which would occur as a gradual annual increase of $500 per child per year until the full $7,000 would be reached in 2016.

McCain has said in the past that the first step to simplifying taxes was to close special interest loopholes. During the 2000 elections, McCain endorsed a middle class tax cut and the expansion of the 15% tax bracket. He said then that we should not promise tax cuts from future surpluses we might not have. It was a widely known fact that the Bush tax cut favored Americans who earn over $1 million dollars per year. This may have been a deterrent in the 2008 elections in voters believing that McCain would provide adequate tax cuts for middle-class Americans, since both men were Republicans with similar beliefs and agendas. The voting public was never quite sure that McCain could be trusted to provide adequate tax cuts for middle class Americans because his ideologies were so similar to those of President Bush. McCain has stated that he believes taxes should be low, simple, and fair and has suggested that the Alternative Minimum Tax be permanently repealed. He has also endorsed making the Bush income and investment tax cuts permanent. He believes that in order to raise taxes, Congress should require a 3/5 majority vote, thus making it much more difficult.

Health Care: Barack Obama

Noting that 45 million Americans lack adequate health coverage because of the excessive cost of it, Obama promised to sign a health care reform plan into law by the end of his first term in office. His plan would provide affordable, accessible health care coverage options for every American. This would be an accomplishment that no other president has been able to achieve in spite of the grave need. Obama stated that too little was spent on prevention and public health, reminding everyone of the epidemic of obesity in US, even among children. He supports more spending in the areas of bio-terrorism and pandemic flu. His solution was to make an up-front investment of $50 billion in electronic health information technology systems to reduce errors, save lives and money.

Obama's plan would also lower the cost of health care and reduce an average family's premiums by around $2,500 per year. For those Americans who currently have health insurance, nothing would change except the lowering of premiums. Those who do not have health insurance would have a range of private insurance options, which would be accessible through a new National Health Insurance Exchange, similar to what Members of Congress currently have.

Obama has suggested many reforms to the current insurance industry such as, reducing the cost of catastrophic illnesses for employers and their employees by reimbursing employers for a portion of costs if savings were used to lower worker's premiums. He has also proposed the reform of medical malpractice and disease management programs that focus on preventive care.

Health Care: John McCain

McCain suggested putting healthcare records online in order to reduce costs and eliminate errors. He supports tax-free Medical Savings Accounts as well as matching funds for senior citizen's prescription drugs. McCain endorsed giving a $5,000 refundable tax credit to families so they would be able to afford to purchase their own insurance plan, saying that families should make their own health and insurance decisions; not the government. He has made statements about keeping health care promises to aging veterans and he supports patient rights including appeal mechanisms when claims are denied and the right to sue when claims are denied. He has stated that there should be more community health centers and walk-in clinics. He has also suggested higher taxes on cigarettes and the regulation of nicotine as a drug and has voted YES on increasing tobacco restrictions. He endorses limits on malpractice lawsuits. McCain would give tax credits to individuals and small businesses to offset insurance costs. In interviews, he has stated that we should bring together "smart Americans" to solve our problems with Medicare. He supports the re-importation of prescription drugs from Canada. His favorite cause is cleft palate surgery for children.

In the NAACP Convention in 2008, McCain said, "We will offer every individual and family a large tax credit to buy their health care, so that their health insurance is theirs to keep even when they move or change jobs."

McCain failed to mention that, under his plan, workers would be taxed on the value of any health benefits paid for by their employers, which isn't the case under current law.

Gun Control: Barack Obama

Obama believes that states and cities should decide local gun laws. He believes in using a common sense approach when enforcing gun licensing laws. He respects the 2nd Amendment but believes we should limit gun purchases to one per month. Obama supports a ban on semi-automatic weapons but believes that retired police officers should be able to carry concealed weapons. He voted against a bill, which would have allowed the illegal use of handguns in a home invasion. Though he believes that laws should be tightened to keep guns out of inner cities, he believes that violence is more a problem of morality. He would go after unscrupulous gun dealers who put weapons in the hands of the mentally ill, convicted criminals or juveniles. Obama believes in increasing state restrictions on the purchase and possession of firearms and he would require that manufacturers provide child-safety locks on all firearms.

During the Democratic debate in 2008, when asked about licensing and registering gun owners, he replied, "I don't think that we can get that done. But what we can do is to provide just some common-sense enforcement. The efforts by law enforcement to obtain the information required to trace back guns that have been used in crimes to unscrupulous gun dealers. As president, I intend to make it happen. We essentially have two realities, when it comes to guns, in this country. You've got the tradition of lawful gun ownership. It is very important for many Americans to be able to hunt, fish, take their kids out, teach them how to shoot. Then you've got the reality of 34 Chicago public school students who get shot down on the streets of Chicago. We can reconcile those two realities by making sure the Second Amendment is respected and that people are able to lawfully own guns, but that we also start cracking down on the kinds of abuses of firearms that we see on the streets."

Gun Control: John McCain

McCain always voted against tightening restrictions on guns purchases at gun shows and in the past has voted to loosen restrictions and background checks. He has also voted YES on prohibiting lawsuits against gun manufacturers and does not believe that gun manufacturers should be held responsible for crimes committed with the weapons they manufacture. Although McCain supports the ban of some assault weapons, overall he opposes restrictions on most assault weapons and ammunition. He voted against the Brady Bill and assault weapons ban in 1999. He supports the ban on the sale of cheap guns and guns without trigger locks and supports allowing guns in national parks. If elected, McCain said that he would: repeal federal restrictions on the purchase and possession of firearms by law-abiding citizens be in favor of allowing citizens to carry concealed firearms

In interviews, McCain admitted that guns contribute to violence but points out that violent web sites and videos are also a problem. He is quoted as saying that gun control is a proven failure in the fight against violent crimes. His proposed, "Youth Violence Prevention Act" would: Prevent juveniles from illegal access to weapons and punish anyone helping them to do so. Prohibit juveniles who commit acts of gun violence from being able to purchase guns in the future. Punish juveniles who carry and use handguns in schools. Sentence juveniles convicted of violent crimes under adult guidelines.

Abortion: Barack Obama

On the abortion issue, Obama has stated that he is not sure if life begins at conception and believes that Americans can find common ground between pro-life and pro-choice. He has opposed legislation that would protect a baby who was born alive because of a failed abortion. He does, however, believe that states should be allowed to restrict late-term partial-birth abortions if they choose. He stated throughout the elections that he would protect a woman's "right to choose" if elected president. He believes that we should educate teens on abstinence and provide contraceptives to reduce unwanted pregnancies. He supports Roe vs. Wade. He voted NO on notifying the parents of teens who would obtain out-of-state abortions.

He is in favor of expanding the stem cell research program, saying that we owe it to the future of our nation to discover what we can in this area. In a 2007 interview, he promised the American people that he would: Promote embryonic Stem Cell Research, Support Medical Advancement and Innovation, Expand the Number of Stem Cell Lines Available for Research, Ensure Ethical Standards.

Abortion: John McCain

Mc Cain has gone on record saying that he is in favor of re-pealing Roe vs. Wade except in the cases of incest or rape. That is in direct contrast to a statement he made in August 1999. At that time, McCain told the San Francisco Chronicle that he would "not support repeal of Roe vs Wade because it would force women to undergo illegal operations." In another inter-view in August 2007, when asked whether he felt national se-curity was a more critical issue that abortion, he answered, "I think the respect and commitment to the rights of the unborn is something I've fought for, and it has a lot to do with national security. Because it says very much what kind of a country we are and our respect for human life, whether it be here in the US or anyplace else in the world. So I think it is connected." He also believes that parents have a right to be involved in their child's decision to abort a baby, saying there should be a "family conference" before any action is taken. In one inter-view, McCain proclaimed, "I am proud of my pro-life record in public life, and I will continue to maintain it. I will not draw my children into this discussion. As a leader of a pro-life party with a pro-life position, I will persuade young Americans [to] understand the importance of the preservation of the rights of the unborn."

He does not believe that the government should fund abor-tions. He has stated that he is pro-life and an advocate for the rights of mankind everywhere. He does, however, support fed-eral funding of embryonic stem cell research. In 2005, McCain voted NO on a bill to reduce teen pregnancy by education and contraceptives. In the past, he has voted against partial birth abortions and military base abortions. In 2008, he voted YES on allowing an unborn child to be eligible for the State Chil-dren's Health Insurance Program.

Social Security: Barack Obama

Obama does not believe that it is fair to seniors to raise the retirement age. He believes that the government has a responsibility to them to be honest about the long-term solvency of the
Social Security Program and ways we can address the shortfall.
His plan to make Social Security more solvent is to ask those
making over $250,000 per year to contribute 2 to 4 per cent
more toward Social Security. He believes these additional contributions will go a long way towards making certain there is
money there for retiring seniors. This message appealed to the
baby boomers, those Americans who were born between 1946
and 1964. According to census figures, there are over 70 million
baby boomers and most of them are now at retirement age. For
years, this generation has been warned that there might not be
social security benefits available to them once they are ready to
retire. This has caused a great amount of fear and resentment
in the baby boomer generation because they have worked hard
all their lives, paid their taxes and social security payments and
feel that they have a right to expect the government to provide retirement benefits to them at retirement age. The Obama
message of change offered them some hope for the future and
gave them the feeling that someone in government cared about
their situation.

Obama and Biden also believe there is a great need to reform Corporate Bankruptcy laws so that workers are higher on
the list of debts that a corporation can not discard. In the past,
bankruptcy courts have demanded more from workers than executives and these practices must be changed. Obama does not
believe it's fair for businesses to issue executive bonuses while
cutting worker's pensions. His plan would increase the amount
of unpaid wages and benefits that a worker can claim in court.
The Obama/Biden plan would require full disclosure of investments made by a company. This information would provide
retirees important resources to make their pension fund more
secure. He does not believe we should privatize social security
but does suggest allowing an earnings cap over $97,500.

Another popular but controversial proposal would be to

eliminate Income Taxes for those seniors who earn less than $50,000. This provides an immediate tax cut of around $1,400 for 7 million seniors, as well as relieving millions of seniors from the burden of filing tax returns.

Social Security: John McCain

McCain jokingly said that more people believe Elvis being alive, than receiving social security benefits. He does, however, believe that the problems and shortfalls in the social security program can be fixed with a bipartisan effort. Some of his proposals to fix the problems are: Personal Savings Accounts, Option to invest 20% of payroll taxes in private accounts, Disallow using Trust Funds for "emergency" spending, eliminate the "earnings test" which taxes benefits; believes the entitlement program must be revamped. In the past, McCain has said that the growth of spending on Medicare threatens our fiscal future and that Republicans and Democrats must sit down together and resolve the many issues that threaten the future of our social security and Medicare programs. He does not believe the job will be difficult once we, as a nation, decide to move forward into some positive solutions.

In a pre-election interview, he was quoted as saying, "We've got a ticking time bomb out there, and it's called the Social Security Trust Fund. And starting in 2014 there'll be more money going out than in. There's a $5 trillion un-funded liability out there in the form of the Social Security Trust Fund. If we can put the money in quick, then we will be able to allow people to invest their payroll taxes into investments of their choosing and make a huge amount of difference in the solvency of their retirement fund." Older Americans felt that, though McCain's proposal had merit, that he did not have the resolve to follow through and make certain these changes were instituted and the Social Security crisis averted.

Foreign Policy: Barack Obama

In 2004, Obama was quoted as saying, "Never has the US had so much power and so little influence to lead." Obama also believes that a president should abide by international human rights treaties and that US policy should always promote democracy and human rights. He believes that it's a disgrace that our leadership has not met with the leadership of enemy governments and that keeping those lines of communication open is essential to having strong relationships worldwide. Obama has been in favor of a "Global Poverty Act", which would allocate 0.7% of the Gross Domestic Product for foreign aid. He has also endorsed $50 billion dollars annually that would strengthen weak states in danger of collapse. Obama believes that America has a moral obligation to intervene in Darfur to avoid spillover and was in favor of sending humanitarian aid there. In 2007, he wrote a law, which would stabilize the Congo with $52 million and has been instrumental in increasing aid to the Congo area. In 2007, he visited the largest slum area in Africa to publicize their plight. He believes that corruption in Africa is a major deterrent to its growth and prosperity. In 2006, he visited Africa to encourage HIV testing and research.

In 2008, Obama endorsed meeting with Cuban leaders and loosening restrictions on the trade embargo there in an effort to mend fences long since decayed between the US and Cuban government. He called the recent Russian actions in Georgia "unacceptable" and believes we should engage Russia regarding nuclear proliferation. He has categorized America's relationship with Russia for the past 8 years as "reactive" and believes that future dealings with them should be "proactive." In 2007, Obama endorsed the strengthening of NATO in order to face 21st century threats around the world.

Foreign Policy: John McCain

McCain has been quoted as saying that he is willing and able to face the threats in this world. He has taken strong military stand against Cuba, saying that America should continue our embargo and indict Castro. He does not believe America should have diplomatic or trade relations with Cuba. He has also endorsed sanctions against Russia until Putin leaves Chechnya. He believes that the problems in Chechnya could spread to the Caucasus oil reserves. He has not been in support of Russian aggression in Georgia. In 2005, he sponsored a bill that would suspend Russia's participation in the G-8. He has been opposed to sending money to Africa for the AIDS epidemic saying that corrupt officials would consume any financial aid sent there. McCain believes that America should overthrow rogue governments in order to protect itself against terrorism and other such threats to our safety.

When asked about the threat of Iran to the world and the Middle East, McCain replied, "If Iran acquires nuclear weapons, it is an existential threat to the State of Israel and to other countries in the region. We cannot have a second Holocaust. Let's just make that very clear. I have proposed a League of Democracies, a group of countries that share common interests, common values, common ideals, they also control a lot of the world's economic power. We could impose significant meaningful, painful sanctions on the Iranians that I think could have a beneficial effect." McCain went on to say that because the government of Iran is weak and poorly organized, their economy is weak as well in spite of having significant oil revenues. He stated that if the French, British, Germans and others nations would come together and unite in an effort to control Iran, it could make a major difference. He ended by saying that he felt Iran would continue on a pathway toward obtaining nuclear weapons and would eventually be a threat to the world.

Immigration: Barack Obama

Obama supports extending welfare and Medicaid benefits to immigrants. He does not believe that deporting them is the answer and that immigration raids are ineffective. He has stated that America has nothing to fear from today's immigrants but that we do need a comprehensive reform in this area. In a 2008 debate, when asked what he would do regarding the many problems that face America concerning illegal aliens, he answered, "For all the noise and anger that too often surrounds the immigration debate, America has nothing to fear from today's immigrants. They have come here for the same reason that families have always come here--for the hope that in America, they could build a better life for themselves and their families. Like the waves of immigrants that came before them and the Hispanic Americans whose families have been here for generations, the recent arrival of Latino immigrants will only enrich our country." He believes America should crack down on employers who hire illegal immigrants and that we need newer, better, more high-tech approaches to patrolling our borders. He is in favor of providing government services in Spanish and encourages every student to learn a second language. He has reminded Americans not to forget that Mexican immigrants are human beings and must be treated with a modicum of respect.

He believes we must help the 12 million undocumented immigrants in our nation get on a responsible path to citizenship, but admits that the immigration bureaucracy is broken and overwhelmed and that this is the major reason why immigrants are forced to come here illegally; because they must wait for years for applications. Obama has suggested working with Mexico to improve their economy as a means of eliminating the need for its people to look for employment elsewhere. In 2008, he supported the DREAM Act, which would provide aid to children of illegal immigrants.

Immigration: John McCain

McCain also wants us to treat illegal aliens with respect, because, as he put it, they are, after all, human beings, while he does not endorse the immediate deportation of all illegal aliens, he does believe that those who commit crimes should be deported. He is in favor of immigrants learning English and has voted YES to English being the official language of the United States government. He believes that immigration reform is essential for the sake of National Security. Though he doesn't support amnesty, he does support temporary worker programs that would allow aliens to work in US. He believes that there are many jobs in America that the average US worker would shun, and that immigrant workers are needed to fill these positions. McCain believes that it is critical for US to shore up and protect its borders and has voted YES on building a fence along the Mexican border. He has also voted YES on allowing illegal aliens to participate in Social Security and YES on the issue of giving work Visas to skilled workers. In the Republican debate of January 2008, McCain denied ever favoring amnesty, saying, "Let me just say I've never supported amnesty." However, in a 2003 interview, he said, "Amnesty has to be an important part because there are people who have lived in this country for 20, 30 or 40 years, who have raised children here and pay taxes here and are not citizens."

In a December 2000 press release, McCain said, "I support the Latino and Immigrant Fairness Act (LIFA). Negotiations between the White House and the leadership, which endorsed more limited immigration reform, have resulted in a compromise. This bill makes meaningful but insufficient progress on amnesty for those wrongly denied it."

The Environment: Barack Obama

Obama promised that America will invest in clean energy and green jobs for the future. His campaign was keen on promoting green technologies and fuel efficiency standards. In April 2008, he was quoted saying that the book of Genesis (from the Christian Bible) teaches humans that we should be good stewards of planet earth. In 1985, he organized the removal of asbestos from a Chicago housing project as well as an inner-city recycling program in October of 2007. He believes in protecting the Great Lakes and our National Parks and forests. He was against giving federal dollars to Halliburton for the rebuilding of New Orleans after the Katrina disaster. He felt that the community would be better served if local contractors were employed to do the necessary work. These comments and opinions were favorably received by local businessmen and women along the Gulf

Coast who agreed with his idea to allow the reconstruction to be done by the people who live in the affected communities. Unlike McCain, Obama was in favor of the formation of a committee to examine the government's slow response to the Katrina disaster.

Obama endorsed a bill to give tax credits for the removal of lead-based paints. He scored 60% on the Humane Society Scorecard for animal protection which was higher than McCain's 40%. In the second presidential debate of 2008, Obama said this: "It is critical that we understand this is not just a challenge, it's an opportunity, because if we create a new energy economy, we can create five million new jobs, easily. It can be an engine that drives us into the future the same way the computer was the engine for economic growth over the last couple of decades. We can do it, but we're going to have to make an investment. The same way the computer was originally invented by a bunch of government scientists who were trying to figure out, for defense purposes, how to communicate, we've got to understand that this is a national security issue as well." Obama's answer was well received by the voting public and seemed to give the people hope for a stronger future, as we all move into the 21st Century. To this same question, McCain simply replied with a standard answer about cleaning up the climate and creating green jobs. His answer lacked the zeal, passion and enthusiasm of Obama's.

The Environment: John McCain

On environmental issues, McCain made many generalized statements. When asked what he would do as president to protect the environment, he answered, "We can move forward, and clean up our climate, and develop green technologies, and alternative energies for battery-powered cars, so that we can clean up our environment and at the same time get our economy going by creating millions of jobs." Though statements like this may sound good, he provides no tangible method to accomplish these tasks. All Americans know that the air, water and soil are polluted. What most are looking to politicians for are some practical ways to accomplish these massive tasks. Obama had some definitive plans for cleaning up the environment and creating "green" jobs at the same time. McCain did not. McCain voted against forming a committee, which would look into the government's failures regarding the Katrina disaster. Many voters believed that he did so because of his allegiance to his good friend, George Bush.

One of McCain's TV ads criticized an earmark that provided $3 million to study the DNA of bears in Montana. In the end though, he voted FOR the proposal. Like Obama, McCain believes that the environmental needs of this country are intricately woven into the economic needs and that if we answer both calls, we can move forward into a future which is not only more prosperous but also includes leaving the heritage of a clean, healthy, beautiful planet to our children. In 1996, he put 3.5 billion acres of land into wilderness protection. He has scored 40 out of a possible 100 on the Human Society Scorecard. He believes we should end commercial whaling and illegal trade in whale meat. In 2002, he was in favor of making the EPA into a Cabinet Department.

Drugs: Barack Obama

In campaign speeches, Obama highlighted the fact that the use of methamphetamines has increased 156% since 1996. He has fought to rid our inner-city neighborhoods of meth labs and supports helping addicts get the healing and deliverance they need in order to live wholesome, productive lives. Obama also supports helping jail inmates who are addicted to methamphetamines get into drug treatment programs. Obama supports allowing non-violent, first-time drug offenders to serve their time in an appropriate drug-rehab clinic instead of jail. He believes this is a more effective tool to rehabilitate drug users. He would provide job training, substance abuse and mental health counseling to ex-offenders, so that they are successfully re-integrated into society. He points out that there is a disparity between sentencing crack and powder-based cocaine and that this policy is wrong and should be completely eliminated.

Obama has been criticized for his honesty in speaking about his own drug use as a teen. He has admitted smoking pot and using cocaine but has denied use of heroine. Most voters were surprised but delighted by his candor. American voters would prefer to have someone honest running their country.

Though Obama is certainly not the first president to use drugs, he holds the distinction of being the first to openly discuss it. In an interview with Jay Leno in 2006, when asked if he had inhaled, Obama replied, "That was the point." His statement pokes fun at the answer given by Bill Clinton in 1992, who admitted to smoking pot as a teen, but stated that he did not inhale. Obama voted against lowering the drinking age from 21 to 18 and believes that in order to help our young people stay away from drugs and alcohol, it is critical for us to discover the reasons why they get involved with those things to begin with.

Drugs: John McCain

McCain stated that the United States is AWOL in the war on drugs. He believes that America should insist that Mexico extradite drug dealers to the US for prosecution and in early 2008, 21 people suspected of drug trafficking between Mexico and the United states were extradited to the USA for trial. Four of those were drug kingpins and, as such, could face the death penalty. In 1999, McCain supported the "Drug Free Borders Act" which would spend $1 billion dollars for better drug detection equipment at the US/Mexico border. He has sponsored a bill that would provide drug testing for major league sports, as well as sponsoring a bill to aid Indian tribes in their fight against methamphetamine use. McCain would increase and expand federally funded drug prevention and treatment programs and he believes that alcohol abuse should be included as well. He has long been in favor of increasing penalties for selling drugs.

In a 1999 speech, McCain said this in regards to maintaining free trade with Mexico, while still restricting the flow of

Obama: First African American President   125

drugs in and out of the United States: "It is a careful balancing act. [We should] ensure that we are doing everything we can to stem the flow of illegal drugs without impeding the flow of legitimate commerce. The key to finding that balance is procuring equipment to expeditiously scan incoming cargo."

Government Reform: Barack Obama

Obama led the battle for political reform in Washington. During his campaign, he refused to accept campaign contributions from PACs and Washington lobbyists. He believes we must close the door between the executive branch and K-Street lobbying shops. He believes that their appointees should serve the American people instead of their own interests. He was in favor of ending wasteful, no-bid government contracts. Obama believes that it's time for government to clean up its act and stop its overall wastefulness. He believes Washington can be run more efficiently; that all ineffective programs need to be eliminated. He supported the reinstatement of PAYGO rules, whereby new government spending would be paid for by cut backs in existing programs. He also promised to protect the Bush tax cuts for the middle class while reversing tax cuts for the wealthy. This was favorably received by middle class Americans, who have long resented the partiality Bush seemed to show to the wealthy.

Obama and Biden promised to stop funding wasteful, obsolete federal government programs that make no financial sense. He called for an end to subsidies to oil and gas companies, who have recorded record profits in the past few years. Also, the elimination of subsidies to the private student loan industry, which has repeatedly used unethical business practices. Obama proposed many innovative reforms in the area of fiscal responsibility. He believes that Washington should set up a system, which would allow the people to track government spending and suggested, "Google for Government" as a name for this program. He suggested that we use current technology to shine the light on federal contracts, earmarks, and proposed bills, thereby allowing the voting public to be involved in policing these spending policies. Obama believes that Cabinet members should hold regular town hall meetings. This innovative approach to problems that have long plagued Washington politics was instrumental in voters believing that Obama would truly make the necessary changes in those troublesome areas where change was and is so desperately needed.

Government Reform: John McCain

On the subject of government reform, McCain holds many strong opinions. In an inspiring speech at the Republican National Convention in September of 2008, McCain had this to say to his supporters: "We need to change the way government does almost everything, from the way we protect our security to the way we compete in the world economy; from the way we respond to disasters to the way we fuel our transportation network; from the way we train our workers to the way we educate our children. All these functions of government were designed before the rise of the global economy, the information technology revolution and the end of the Cold War. We have to catch up to history, and we have to change the way we do business in Washington. The constant partisan rancor that stops us from solving these problems isn't a cause, it's a symptom. It's what happens when people go to Washington to work for themselves and not for you. Again and again, I've worked with members of both parties to fix problems that need to be fixed. That's how I will govern as president. I will reach out my hand to anyone to help me get this country moving again. I have the record and scars to prove it. Obama does not."

His speech was well received by his followers, and though many others before him have made similar promises, still business goes on as usual in Washington. The American people did not feel like McCain had the strong resolve needed to create such radical changes in the way government does business. Though McCain has worked throughout his career to curtail wasteful spending and bring reform to campaign financing, his efforts in these areas have gone largely unnoticed by the American public. He has also been quoted as saying, "Wasteful

spending in Washington has gone from irresponsible to inde-
fensible."

McCain promised to fix broken government programs, reminding voters that even according to the federal government
itself, one-fifth of all government programs do not perform as
they were designed to do.

Education: Barack Obama

One of the more popular proposals Obama made in the area of
education was for the government to pay the entire cost of education for anyone wishing to become a teacher. With so few young
people wishing to devote themselves to four years of college in
order to become a teacher, this seems like a perfect fix. He has
also endorsed an innovative program, which would guarantee
higher education for those who would volunteer in their communities, as well as a $2500 tax credit for those enrolled in four
years of college. He has stated that he is only where he is today
because he was given the opportunity for an excellent education
and that it is wrong to settle for an America where some kids
are not given the opportunity to be all they can be. He would
invest in early childhood education and recruit an army of new
teachers. He would pay these new teachers better salaries and
give them the support they require. In exchange, they will be
held to higher standards and greater accountability.

Obama believes that in order to have a strong future, America must make education a priority. In a state of the Union address in February of 2009, Obama said, "In a global economy
where the most valuable skill you can sell is your knowledge,
a good education is no longer just a pathway to opportunity-
-it is a prerequisite. And yet, we have one of the highest high
school dropout rates of any industrialized nation. And half of
the students who begin college never finish. This is a prescription for economic decline."

In other speeches, Obama has tied the nation's economic
health and wealth to its ability to educate and inspire its children.

Education: John McCain

John McCain said that he does not believe in creationism but does see the hand of God at work in the earth. Those two statements seem contradictory. He has also stated that he believes the individual school districts should make the call about whether or not to teach creationism to their children. He does believe that ethics and virtues should be taught in school. He has endorsed giving pay bonuses or increases to teachers in some of the more troubled school districts. He believes schools should answer to parents and students. He has also endorsed a program that would identify the best teachers and reward them, as well as identifying the worst teachers and helping them to find another line of work. He believes that in order for kids to obtain the very best education, we need qualified teachers who are enthusiastic about their jobs. McCain supports tax-free savings accounts for education expenses. He has also proposed $500 million for the building of virtual schools and to develop online courses for students. He would allocate another $250 million to support state programs expanding education opportunities, including the creation of public virtual charter schools. States would use these funds to build virtual math, and science academies, expand the availability, of Advanced Placement courses, online tutoring and courses in foreign languages.

In July of 2008 at the NAACP, McCain proposed educational reform that would allow parents to choose a tutor or tutoring program for a child that has fallen behind in school and isn't making the grade. He believes that it is counter-productive and not in the best interests of the child to force parents to seek federal aid. Parents should be able to purchase tutoring directly, without having to deal with the same educational system that failed their child in the first place. Needless restrictions like these would be removed. If a student needs extra help, parents would be able to sign them up to get it, with direct public support.

He has been quoted as saying that a good teacher should earn more than a bad lawyer and that it is unconscionable that the average lawyer earns $79,000 per year, while the average teacher only earns $39,000 per year.

Free Trade: Barack Obama

Unlike McCain, Obama feels that America should insist on certain labor and human rights standards when establishing a Free Trade Agreement with another nation. He has also suggested in the past using trade agreements with other nations as a means of promoting democracy in those nations. Obama believes that past presidents have not always had the interests of the American worker and business owner in mind when creating free trade agreements with other nations. In the third presidential debate of 2008, Obama had this to say: "When it comes to South Korea, we've got a trade agreement up right now. They are sending hundreds of thousands of South Korean cars into the US. We can only get 4,000 to 5,000 into South Korea. That is not free trade. We've got to have a president who is going to advocate on behalf of American businesses and American workers and I make no apology for that." In a speech in Berlin in 2008, Obama said that the world must build on the wealth that open markets have created and share its benefits more equitably. He believes that we will not be able to sustain this growth if free trade only favors the few and not the many.

Another critical aspect of Free Trade brought to light by Obama during the 2008 debates was that globalization is here to stay and that we cannot go backwards in regards to industry and commerce. He pointed out that today's workers and businesses in America face competition not only from other companies in the United States, but also from businesses and workers all over the world. These are important factors to bear in mind when planning for 21st century Free Trade Agreements.

Corporations can now cut their operating costs considerably simply by relocating their facilities to other nations. Many larger businesses have already done so, leaving American workers jobless. Obama believes that we must not allow trade policies to be dictated by special interest groups and to do so will erode public support for robust trade. He has spoken out against allowing subsidized and unfairly traded products to flood our markets. In a speech in Flint, Michigan in 2008, he said: "We cannot stand by while countries manipulate currencies to promote exports, creating huge imbalances in the global economy."

Free Trade: John McCain

McCain supports the North American Free Trade Agreement but he does not believe it should include provisions to address environmental concerns or protect worker's rights. He has long been a supporter of the trade embargo against Cuba and believes that it should stay in place in the future. He also supports the General Agreement on Tariffs and Trade, as well as the United States continuing its membership in the World Trade Organization. He believes that free trade has been the engine of our economy and that we should continue strong free trade policies, for they are the principles that guide our nation's economy. McCain has taken a strong stand against subsidies. In December 2007 during the Republican debate he said, "Subsidies are a mistake, and I don't believe anybody can say that they're a fiscal conservative and yet support subsidies which distort markets and destroy our ability to compete in the world, as well as our ability to get cheaper products into the US."

McCain supports free trade with Mexico, and believes we must keep that trade door open in spite of numerous problems with drug trafficking. He is opposed to a tax provision which is basically a corporate tax shelter saving corporations such as McDonalds, Microsoft and Boeing around $4 billion dollars a year in taxes and export duties.   He believes we should lower our barriers and encourage free trade with all nations unless it becomes a security risk to do so. McCain believes that globalization is an opportunity for the future of American workers. He would like the U.S. to engage in multilateral, regional and bilateral efforts to reduce barriers to trade, thus leveling the global playing field. He has been accused of believing that any trade agreement is a good trade agreement.

Energy and Oil: Barack Obama

In a 2008 speech, Obama pointed out that McCain had only met with environmentalists once during a certain period of time. But he had met with Big Oil 43 times during that same time period. This statement fueled the suspicions of American voters who were concerned that, if elected president, McCain would continue to favor Big Oil just as his predecessor had done. Because of huge price spikes in fuel prices over the past few years, Americans by and large detest Big Oil Companies and are aware of former President Bush's close ties to them. The Obama campaign tapped into this undercurrent of hostility among voters and took every possible advantage of it. Obama also pointed out that though America is making some strides toward producing fuel-efficient automobiles, the automobiles themselves are being manufactured in other countries such as, South Korea and Japan. He believes that it is crucial for America to not only develop fuel-efficient and battery-powered autos, but to manufacture them here in America. This works to provide good jobs for Americans and boosts our economy.

Obama believes that the US can be completely dependent of its reliance on foreign oil within ten years. He cited the speech by JFK in the early 60's where he proclaimed to the American public that we would reach the moon within ten years, saying that once Americans set their minds to doing something, they can get it done. Obama has been reluctant to support Nuclear power in the past because of safety concerns, but believes that it has its place in the overall energy mix. He leans more toward supporting the development of wind, solar and geothermal power. One of his major concerns has been the safe disposal of nuclear waste. In a June 2008 interview, Obama accused McCain of wanting to build 45 new nuclear power plants without having a solid plan in place to store the nuclear waste. In the past, Obama has also criticized McCain for his support of a plan that would store nuclear waste at the federal government's Yucca Mountain site in Nevada.

During his campaign, he reminded Americans that domestic oil drilling is a stop-gap measure and not a long-term solution. At some point, those resources will be completely depleted. He also advocates developing clean coal technology as well as natural gas reserves. In a 2007 speech, Obama blamed the political climate in Washington for many of our environmental and energy problems. He stated that corporate special interest groups have too much control in these areas. He said: "We have heard promises to curb our use of fossil fuels in nearly every State of the Union address since the oil embargo of 1973. Our energy problem has become an energy crisis because no matter how well-intentioned the promise, they all fall victim to the same Washington politics that has only become more divided and dishonest; more beholden to the powerful interests that have the biggest stake in the status quo."

Energy and Oil: John McCain

The struggle to free ourselves from dependence on oil from the Middle East has been and is a hot topic for politicians. Though McCain has stated in past interviews that he is for seeking alternative fuel sources, such as wind and solar power, in the past he has voted against alternative energy 11 times. Many have speculated that this is due largely to his close ties with the Bush presidency, which has shown partiality toward Big Oil Companies in the past. McCain struggled to free himself from the doubts and suspicions of US voters concerning whether or not he would closely follow Bush policies should he become president. McCain's voting record seems to indicate that he would be slow in moving to develop alternative fuel sources for America and this is an area where Americans feel there must be change in the near future.

In the minds of many Americans, the war in Iraq is about nothing more than the control of oilfields. More than 75% of Americans believe that the government should increase its efforts in developing alternate energy sources. A question on the mind of many voters prior to the 2008 elections may have been: "Will McCain break away from Bush policies concerning oil and take America in a new and better direction toward developing alternative fuel sources?" With Americans more concerned than ever about Global Warming and climate change, this was certainly a critical factor in deciding the presidency. Americans by and large believe that mankind must reduce its carbon footprint on the earth and begin to work with our ecological systems instead of defying and defiling them.

During a 2008 interview, McCain said that he would work toward building 45 new nuclear power plants by 2030. He believes that nuclear energy is safe and efficient. Obama on the other hand, has been reluctant to get behind such a philosophy because of concerns about safely storing the nuclear waste that is produced by nuclear reactors. Overall, the Obama campaign endorsed green, clean energy and a more progressive move toward alternate fuel sources, while the McCain campaign supported continuing to rely on oil from the Middle East along with nuclear power. Though support towards nuclear energy has gradually increased over the past 10 years, 77% of Americans favor increased government spending to develop alternative energy sources.

Homeland Security: Barack Obama

In a 2007 interview, when asked about his lack of experience in areas such as the war and terrorism, Obama replied that he felt that good, sound judgment was just as vital as experience. He does not sanction torture under any circumstances and has stated that Homeland Security should protect its citizens instead of invading their privacy. He also endorsed closing Guantanamo and restoring the right of habeas corpus. In March of 2007, he was quoted as saying, "America must practice the patriotism it preaches" and that personal privacy must be protected even in an age of terrorism. He believes that we should increase the size of our military so that those in war zones can be rotated out at regular intervals. He would give the US military the very best training and equipment available. He believes that America must not only be strong, but that we must use wisdom as well to defeat our enemies. Concerning terrorism, he believes that Al Qaeda is stronger now than it was in 2001 because America has been distracted by the war in Iraq. He has stated that our invasion of Afghanistan is the major reason that America has not been attacked again as it was on 9/11. He believes that the attacks in Afghanistan disrupted and weakened Al Qaeda and he supports that invasion.

When asked about America's moral obligation to intervene when it sees injustice around the world, he answered that, though we do have a moral obligation to step in when we witness horrific acts of violence such as genocide, there is a great amount of cruelty in the world and it will not be possible for America to get involved in every dispute. He has criticized the cost of high-tech weapons which are not being used, such as the F-22 Raptor. The F-22 Raptor, which costs $140 million dollars, is a high-tech fighter plane that has been operational since 2005 but has never been used in combat. Obama believes that the President of the United States must obey the laws and that illegal surveillance, even for the cause of national security, should not be allowed. He has stated that any American citizen, who is being detained for questioning as an enemy combatant, should be allowed access to counsel and fair procedure. He does not believe that human rights should be sacrificed in the interests of National Security. In many interviews he has made it clear that as president he will work at opening the lines of communication with our enemies and that this is a basic necessity in resolving issues between nations.

Homeland Security: John McCain

In a straw poll debate in 2007, McCain said this:

"I firmly believe that the challenge of the 21st century is the struggle against radical Islamic extremism. It is a transcendent issue. It is hydra-headed. It will be with us for the rest of the century. I have served my nation and my country and the people of this country for all of my adult life. I am the most prepared. I have been involved in these issues. I have served this nation in the military and in the Congress, and I'm the best prepared and need no on-the-job training to meet that challenge." That "struggle" has included years of futile efforts to locate and punish Osama Bin Laden. In answer to questions regarding how he would capture Bin Laden, McCain has said that America needs to establish an organization similar to the OSS in World War II. He believes that we must train tough, smart spies and commission them to go and do whatever necessary to find Bin Laden and bring him to justice. Even though he is against torturing detainees, McCain has made it very clear that he was against the Supreme Court decision establishing habeas corpus for Guantanamo detainees. He called the ruling, "One of the worst decisions in the history of this country." Siding with Supreme Court Justice, Antonin Scalia, he predicted that it would cause more Americans to be killed. A Pentagon "Fact Sheet" dated June of 2008 showed that 37 former Guantanamo detainees are confirmed or suspected of having returned to terrorist activities, which supports McCain's predictions.

In various statements, McCain has credited President Bush for keeping America safe from any more attacks on American soil, such as the terrorist attack of 9/11. He also supported the president's pre-emptive strike on Iraq, saying that America has a right to defend herself if she feels threatened. Regarding the war in Iraq, McCain believes that we should see it through to its successful conclusion. He does not believe in ending the war based on public outcry or opinion and that to do so would be an injustice to those who have fought and died there. He believes we must honor the sacrifices already made there and as a nation, stay firmly resolved to win. In spite of these strong stances in support of the war, directly after the 9/11 tragedy, McCain argued in favor of closing unnecessary military bases across the United States. He also supports allowing gays to serve in the military. He believes that women have shown skill, courage and heroism in combat situations and should not be restricted from serving in the armed forces.

Crime: Barack Obama

Obama believes that the way to reduce the crime rate is to provide job training for criminals so that they are not as likely to return to criminal activities. He would also provide drug and mental health counseling for offenders. In a speech delivered to the NAACP in 2008, he said: "We have to fight for those young men standing on street corners with little hope for the future besides ending up in jail. We have to break the cycle of poverty and violence that's gripping too many neighborhoods." He also believes we need more law enforcement out on the streets, as well as tougher laws and penalties for violent crimes, but that the root of the problem lies in our families. Obama believes that strong families where both parents are present to help with the raising of our youth is the surest way to reduce crime.

Obama supports fairness in the criminal justice system and believes that we must end all racial profiling. In a February 2008 speech, he cites statistics which show that blacks and Hispanics are more than twice as likely to be stopped and searched by the police. He has stated that by the end of his first four years in office, he would like to see more African Americans youths in college than in jails. Obama believes that the civil rights division of the criminal justice department should be aggressive in investigating hate crimes. He supports the increasing and strengthening of hate crimes legislation. As a US Senator, he has a strong record in the area of civil liberties and has successfully sponsored legislation to combat racial profiling.   In 2002, he pushed for a bill in Illinois, which would mandate the videotaping of all interrogations as a means of curtailing police abuse during interviews. He has admitted that Chicago is well known for use of torture by police to help frame innocent people. Thirteen innocent men on Death Row were exonerated and released, some of them victims of these tortured confessions. He believes that something must be done to restore the public's confidence in the police. While he does not support the death penalty, Obama does admit that certain heinous crimes against people, especially children, warrant the ultimate punishment.

Crime: John McCain

Just as his predecessor, George Bush, McCain supports the death penalty and even believes that the scope and usage of the death penalty should be broadened. He would also like to see stricter penalties for violent felons. He does, however, support job-training programs for those incarcerated. He also supports drug and alcohol rehab programs for prison inmates.

He has endorsed the "Truth in Sentencing" program, which mandates that certain convicted criminals serve their entire sentence and not be released early. He believes that funding should be increased so that communities are able to hire more police officers. In regards to juvenile crimes, McCain believes that in most cases, under-age perpetrators of violent crimes should be held to the same laws and standards as adult criminals. He does, however, believe they should be incarcerated in a separate facility from adult offenders and receive the appropriate remedial and rehabilitation services. He supports the use of "boot camps" for certain juvenile offenders as a means of rehabilitating them. He also believes in job training programs for "at-risk" youth, as well as job placement programs. McCain recognizes the good work of Boys and Girls Clubs, as well as other youth organizations in our communities and believes that the government should increase funding for these organizations that are working with at-risk youth. McCain supports increasing the penalty for any violent crime committed on school grounds.

In a speech in 1999, McCain urged the FBI to hold hearings to determine what could be done to prevent and more effectively deal with "hate crimes", saying that any violent act against a citizen perpetrated simply because of race, ethnic or religious beliefs is especially abhorrent. McCain co-sponsored the Sexual Offender Tracking and Identification Act, which establishes a national database at the FBI of criminal offenses against minors or sexual crimes of any nature. This act requires sexual offenders to register with the FBI. They must register their current address, work place information, and have their fingerprints on file with the state where they reside for a period of at least 10 years. In cases where an offender has been convicted of more than one sexual offense, their information must be kept current with the FBI and state authorities for as long as they live.

Civil Rights : Barack Obama

One of the most controversial topics of the 21st Century has been same sex marriage. In the state of California, Proposition 8, an amendment to the state constitution, passed in the general elections of November 4, 2008. Proposition 8 changed the state constitution to restrict the definition of marriage to opposite sex couples and eliminated marriage between same-sex couples, thereby overriding portions of the ruling of In Re Marriage Cases. The amendment added the following wording: "Only marriage between a man and a woman is valid or recognized in California." On the issue of same sex marriages, both candidates kept a low profile, choosing not to be excessively vocal on this hot topic, however, on the whole, Democrats support allowing gays to marry and this was the stance that Obama took as well. Most political analysts did not feel that the positions of each candidate on this issue affected the outcome of the election to any significant degree.

Regarding the issues of race, Obama believes that America must move beyond the old prejudices and racial issues and begin to work together to solves some of the nation's biggest problems, such as immigration. He has worked with Latino leaders for the past 20 years to repair our broken system of immigration. He believes that America is a nation of immigrants and that once we learn to work together, our differences can actually make us stronger. Since Obama is himself African American, his message was well-received by the voting public but only time will tell if long-held racial prejudices can be discarded in favor of a stronger, more united America. During 2007, Obama was asked about the NAACP's current position regarding the flying of the Confederate Flag over the statehouse in North Carolina. He replied that the flag belonged in a museum and should not be flown over a federal building. The NAACP has asked tourists, events and sporting groups not to come to North Carolina until the Confederate Flag has been removed.

Civil Rights: John McCain

In 2008, McCain went on record in support of Proposition 8 in California, saying, "I support the efforts of the people of California to recognize marriage as a unique institution between a man and a woman, just as we did in my home state of Arizona." On the issue of allowing gays into the military, the "Don't ask, don't tell" policy, McCain was quoted as saying that he believes the policy is working just fine and could see no reason to tamper with it. In the past, he has stated that he believes that gay marriage is an issue best left to each individual state to decide for them and not something the federal government should police. In general, he does not believe employers should discriminate against gays when hiring.

During his campaign, the press brought to light that in 1983, McCain voted against making Martin Luther King Jr.'s birthday a federal holiday. McCain was also asked about his voting against civil rights legislation in 1990. Some felt that he would not be able to reach minority voters because of his past voting record on these topics and issues. In an interview in April of 2008, McCain apologized for his opposition to the 1983 vote, saying that we all make mistakes and that he was wrong to oppose the legislation making MLK's birthday a federal holiday.

Regarding the treatment of American Indians, McCain has long felt that the treatment of the Indians is, "One of the darker chapters of the American people." He has expressed great dismay at the horrible conditions on many of the nation's Indian reservations, especially the Sioux Reservation in South Dakota. He has also criticized the rigid rules of bureaucracy on many reservations, highlighting one restriction, which stifles free enterprise by forcing people to wait 2 or 3 years to begin a new business.

McCain is in favor of religious expression on public school property. In a speech in 2000, he said, "School prayer or a moment of silence should be allowed but not mandated. Education is a civil rights issue. Education reform, including school choice is necessary so every student can be prepared for success in higher education, career and life." On the issue of allowing the Ten Commandments to be posted outside federal buildings or taught in school, McCain believes that the Ten Commandments are virtues, which can only enhance a person's walk through life. Ideals and philosophies such as, "Do not murder" and "Do not steal" are values that we, as Americans, should all support.

During the 1999 controversy over the state of North Carolina flying a Confederate Flag over its state capital, McCain said that he believed the Confederate Flag represents the heritage of a people, but that it should not be flown over a state capital building. He also believes that each individual state should decide for itself whether or not to allow such things.

Welfare and Poverty: Barack Obama

Obama approached the welfare and poverty issues with fresh, new ideas. One of those is the creation of 20 "Promise Neighborhoods". In this program, 20 neighborhoods would be built across America in areas with high levels of poverty and crime and low levels of academic achievement. These neighborhoods would be modeled after the Harlem Children's Zone, which provides early childhood education, youth violence prevention and after-school programs. These benefits and programs for the poor would be available to children from birth to college. On the matter of poverty, Obama has said that it doesn't matter if you can sit in the front of the bus if you don't have the money for the fare and it doesn't matter if you can sit at the lunch counter if you are unable to purchase a meal.

Obama has a record of engaging people of faith on all aspects of his public service. His first job out of college was bringing churches together to help address the pressing problems of Chicago's poorest neighborhoods. After Hurricane Katrina, Obama brought together relief organizations and churches to discuss rebuilding the Gulf Coast. He also passed legislation that saved tithing from bankruptcy courts. In June 2006, he delivered what a Washington Post columnist called "perhaps the most important speech on religion and politics in 40 years".

Speaking before an evangelical audience, Senator Obama candidly discussed his own Christian faith and the need for a deeper, more substantive conversation about the role of faith in American life. In December of 2006, Obama joined Pastor Rick Warren to discuss moral leadership and Global AIDS. In June of 2007, Obama challenged Americans to come together around a "Politics of Conscience" in order to move our nation forward into the 21st century.

Welfare and Poverty: John McCain

John McCain believes that helping the poor is a responsibility for communities as well as the government. In a speech in 2000, he said, "Welfare and anti-poverty assistance is a shared responsibility among federal, state and local government; the private sector; community and faith-based organizations. Welfare policy must provide a strong safety net, while promoting work, responsibility, self sufficiency and dignity." Although McCain supports housing assistance for low-income families, he believes that those on welfare have an obligation to work and/or attend some type of training program. He supports continued Medicaid benefits for those who were once on Welfare but have been able to get jobs and move on with their lives. He also supports increased funding for childcare programs.

McCain believes that providing some type of apartment voucher to the homeless would make it possible for them to get off the streets and into homes of their own. In 1999, he sponsored the "Urban Homestead Act" (S.485), which would publish a list of unoccupied multifamily housing projects, substandard housing projects, and other residential property owned by the federal government (HUD), and transfer ownership to corporations requesting them. McCain supports innovative approaches to helping the poor get jobs and get on their feet, such as providing federal assistance to low-income job applicants who need transportation in order to get to their jobs but do not have public transportation available to them. He has also suggested providing tax incentives to companies who would hire and train the homeless, as well as tax credits for companies that would move into areas with high unemployment rates. He believes that converting government funded low-income housing projects into private housing and allowing the residents to run them would strengthen these communities and the families that live in them.

Technology: Barack Obama

One of the most innovative ideas Obama has endorsed is "Google for Government". In a bipartisan effort he worked alongside Republican, Tom Coburn, to create an easy way for the public to track government spending. Obama believes that this plan will encourage healthier fiscal responsibility. Obama has stated that the Bush administration lacked the foresight to invest the necessary monies in research and development so that America could continue to lead the world in pioneering inventions and groundbreaking technologies. For this reason, he has promised to double the federal government's funding for basic research. He also believes that we should make the R&D tax credit permanent in order to encourage businesses to move forward in this area.

In a speech in 2008, Obama stated that America's infrastructure is crumbling, citing the findings of the American Society of Civil Engineers, who gave our national infrastructure, i.e. America's roads and bridges, a "D". He would launch a National Infrastructure Reinvestment Bank, which would invest $60 billion dollars over a ten-year period in improvements to our infrastructure. This act would also create many new jobs.

Concerning Internet usage and technologies, Obama believes America can lead the way in an effort to provide broadband access to every community no matter how remote. He would do this through a combination of reform to the Universal Service Fund and better use of the nation's wireless spectrum, as well as promoting next-generation facilities, technologies and applications. He also believes that new tax and loan incentives will move America forward in this arena. The Obama campaign generated much more interest on social networking sites than any other politician in history. Obama's

MySpace page reached 160,000 people. An Obama Facebook page had over 200,000 supporters within 2 weeks. Joe Trippi, Howard Dean's Internet campaign manager, observed, "It took our campaign 6 months to get 139,000 people on an email list. It took one Facebook group barely a month to get to 200,000. That's astronomical." At another event, Obama drew thousands to a university rally organized online by students using Facebook. Obama hadn't even met the student organizers until he arrived at the event. By March 2007, just a few weeks after Obama began his campaign, his website, "MyBarackObama.com", had attracted over 3,000 volunteer groups, 4,400 personal fundraising pages, and over 6,000 blogs. This effort concluded with some 38,000 people supporting the Obama campaign in their online profiles and through social networking sites. This new age of decentralized politics takes much of the power out of the hands of political consultants and lays it into the hands of individuals. Obama has recognized this power as a force to be utilized in years to come to aid in growing our nation in a variety of ways.

Technology: John McCain

In a February 2008 speech, McCain said, "We must make a farsighted, robust, and fervent commitment to innovation and new technologies to sustain our global competitiveness, meet our national security challenges, achieve less costly and more effective health care, reduce dangerous dependence on foreign sources of oil, and raise the quality of education in the United States." One of the "farsighted approaches" he spoke of was the ban on new cell phone taxes. He believes that this is the future of communications and that we must begin now to address issues such as taxing phone calls and text messages.

McCain also believes that in order to stay competitive in the world, we should offer a permanent R&D Tax Credit. He stated that innovation is fueled by access to sufficient risk capital, a light regulatory burden and skilled workers. He believes that a permanent Tax Credit is sufficient incentive to urge corporations, as well as individuals to reach out and expand in this area. He does not support taxing Internet commerce, saying that this would only serve to curtail the development of business opportunities through the Internet. He believes that the Internet tax moratorium should be made permanent.

Families and Children: Barack Obama

Obama's message concerning families was a strong one. His own devotion and commitment to his family was noticeable. It had the ring of sincerity. Americans witnessed and watched his interaction with his family and in the end, this was a powerful determining factor in his being elected to president of the United States. Americans believe in family. They believe that strong families make a strong nation. In spite of the demanding task of a presidential election, Obama appeared to stay close to his.

In a speech at the NAACP in 2008, Obama said, "If we're serious about reclaiming the American dream, we have to do more in our own lives, our own families, and our own communities. That starts with providing the guidance our children need, turning off the TV, and putting away the video games; attending those parent-teacher conferences, helping our children with their homework, and setting a good example. It starts with teaching our daughters to never allow images on television to tell them what they are worth; and teaching our sons to treat women with respect, and to realize that responsibility does not end at conception; that what makes them men is not the ability to have a child but the courage to raise one. It starts by being good neighbors and good citizens who are willing to volunteer in our communities--and to help our synagogues and churches and community centers feed the hungry and care for the elderly. We all have to do our part to lift up this country."

Obama supports paid sick days and better family leave so that an employee does not have to choose between keeping their job and caring for a sick child or ailing parent. He has endorsed the expansion of the Family and Medical Leave Act. He has committed himself to creating a committee that would encourage businesses to allow employees to participate in Flex-

ible Work Opportunities. He endorses the expansion of Flex-
ible Work Arrangements, thus making it possible for workers
to work at home during at least a portion of their workweek.
He also supports removing the financial penalty on married
couples that file taxes jointly. He believes we should reward fathers who choose to pay their child support and be responsible
regarding their duties as a father. He believes that parents have
a responsibility to police the programs their children watch on
television each week as well as limiting their access to certain
web content.

Obama co-sponsored the White House Conference on Children and Youth in 2010 Act. This act directs the President to call
a White House Conference on Children and Youth in 2010 in
order to encourage improvements in each state and local child
welfare system, as well as develop recommendations for actions
that can be taken to implement policy regarding federal, state,
and local programs which would extend aid to children.

Families and Children: John McCain

McCain supports giving federal tax incentives to families to
help them save for college. He also believes that the government
should encourage employers to offer flextime work schedules
to their employees, along with comp-time and unpaid leave for
family emergencies. He supports low-income housing for the
poor. He has stated that allowing our children to have unfil-
tered access to the Internet robs them of their innocence. He
believes that parents have a responsibility to be aware of what
their kids are watching on TV and on the internet, although he
admits that he doesn't always know what his kids are doing online. Right after the Littleton School shooting, McCain, along
with three other lawmakers, wrote to then President Clinton
calling for a "closer look at the entertainment media and the
violent images and messages with which they are bombard-
ing our children." McCain has stated that parents need clear,
consistent information about the entertainment products that
they are purchasing.

McCain has issued an appeal to Hollywood, calling for a "new social compact" which would remind parents of their responsibilities in deciding the entertainment media that their children are allowed to view. In an interview concerning media violence, McCain said, "Our homes are being flooded by a tide of media violence. As concerns grow over the climate of violence in our culture today, it's important not only for parents to take a greater role in their children's lives but also to encourage the industry to be responsible citizens." He supports a labeling system on movies, video games and music. The "21st Century Media Responsibility Act" would amend the Cigarette Labeling Act to apply its warning label requirements to violent media products. "Our children are vulnerable to images of violence. We must help parents better determine the violent content of the entertainment products by giving them information," McCain said. In 1999, McCain voted against an amendment, which would prohibit the distribution of violent video programming into homes during the hours when children are most likely to comprise a substantial portion of the viewing audience.

McCain has an 83% rating from the Christian Coalition regarding family issues. The Christian Coalition was formed in 1989 by evangelist, Pat Robertson, to help inform families of faith concerning such things as violence in the media. It also gives the Christian community a unified voice in government.

Corporations: Barack Obama

One of the most heated discussions during the presidential race was taxes. McCain accused Obama of wanting to raise taxes but in the end, it was McCain whose tax breaks would have favored that top 5% of the very wealthy corporations, such as Exxon Mobil. These companies, by the way, were the ones given numerous benefits over the course of the eight years Bush was in office. Obama claimed that an independent study showed his tax plan package would provide 3 times the tax relief to middle class Americans and those middle class Americans were more disposed to believe what he was saying than McCain's message.

This was another instance where the mere fact that McCain was a Republican and friend of George Bush caused voters to believe Obama's message over McCain's. Obama also promised that there would be no capital gains tax on earnings under $250,000 and this idea appealed to the millions of small business owners in America. During the first presidential debate in 2008, McCain stated that the United States has the second highest corporate tax rate of any country in the world, which is 35% and that this fact has been a major cause of corporations moving their facilities overseas. However, during that same debate, Obama made the point that there are so many loopholes in the corporate tax code that often, US businesses pay much less than businesses in other countries.

Obama touched on another subject, which was very near and dear to the heart of voters. At the NAACP Convention in 2008, he said, "When CEOs are making more in ten minutes than the average worker earns in a year, and millions of families lose their homes due to unscrupulous lending, checked neither by a sense of corporate ethics or a vigilant government; when the dream of entering the middle class and staying there is fading for young people in our community, we have more work to do." Most Americans were and are disgusted with the status quo in corporate America. Polls show that Americans are sick of hearing that some CEO of a large corporation has just given himself a huge raise while dozens were being laid-off. Middle class Americans believe that politicians and corporate executives should abide by the same laws and ethics as the rest of the nation. Obama believes that corporations should not get billions of dollars in tax deductions if they move overseas. He promised to fight to ensure that public contracts are awarded to those companies who would remain committed to American workers.

Many of Obama's beliefs and campaign promises favored the middle-class, a segment of society that was largely overlooked and forgotten about during the 8 year Bush presidency. Some of the most critical of those were: Obama joined union efforts to get Wal-Mart and other large employers to improve working conditions, wages and health coverage. He supported amending bankruptcy laws to keep companies from avoiding their pension obligations. He supported new rules to force companies to properly fund their pension plans so that workers aren't left without adequate retirement security. He voted to shore up the funding of the Pension Benefit Guaranty Corporation. Another innovative proposal developed by the Obama campaign was something called, "REAL USA". The REAL stands for Responsible, Accountable, Loyal and his plan would reward companies that create quality jobs in America with tax incentives. There were certain stipulations and requirements that had to be met in order for corporations to be eligible for these tax incentives, but the plan had merit.

Corporations: John McCain

While McCain supported the $786 billion dollar bailout, he reminded voters that long ago he warned the public about Fannie Mae and Freddie Mac. He also brought up issues concerning corporate greed and waste. In a 2008 speech, he had this to say, "A lot of us saw this train wreck coming. But there's also the issue of responsibility. President Eisenhower, on the night before the Normandy invasion, went into his room, and wrote out two letters. One of them was a letter congratulating the great members of the military and Allies that had conducted and succeeded in the greatest invasion in history--still, to this day, and forever. And he wrote out another letter, and that was a letter of resignation from the US Army for the failure of the landings at Normandy. Somehow we've lost that accountability. I've been heavily criticized because I called for the resignation of the chairman of the Securities and Exchange Commission. We've got to start also holding people accountable, and we've got to reward people who succeed."

In another speech, McCain seemingly contradicted himself by saying that he believes that the fundamentals of our economy are sound. However, he feels that America needs a stricter interpretation of the various regulatory agencies. He feels that in order for our economy to be so troubled at this time, many of those regulatory systems that were set in place to protect us were not doing their job. He added that he believes in the goodness and strength of the American worker and that they are the most productive workers on the planet. McCain has stated that government should lend a helping hand to American businesses and do all possible to support their success instead of getting in their way. He supports cutting the corporate tax rate from 35% to 25%. On the issue of establishing permanent tax credits on the money a company spends on R&D, he sides with Obama and believes that these tax cuts should equal 10 per cent of the wages spent. He believes that tax cuts and incentives such as these will eventually make American businesses and hence, the economy, much stronger.

Principles and Values: Barack Obama

On issues of principles and values, Obama was, throughout the campaign, suspected of having ties to radical Muslims. There were even rumors that he was one. He was also tied to people of questionable background such as Bill Ayers, the co-founder of "Weather Underground", the violent radical group responsible for bombings of public buildings in the 60's and 70's.

These issues came up again and again throughout the race and were extensively discussed online at various blogging and social networking sites. In the last presidential debate of 2008, McCain again brought up Obama's questionable relationship with Bill Ayers to which Obama adamantly replied that he had many associates in a variety of fields with whom he had contact and/or business but that he was in no way, "friends" with Ayers. Bill Ayers himself said that he and Obama were nothing more than neighbors and family friends, which seems to contradict Obama's statement.

In any other presidential race, these associations with known communists and violent radicals would have been enough to shift the flow to the other party. This was not the case however, in the 2008 elections. One factor may have been that young American voters had no idea who Bill Ayers and the Weather Underground were. The other main factor was Obama himself. He was different than most other presidential candidate. He was younger. He was black. He had radical ideas for changing America. The American public was consistently ready to forgive him of just about anything and overlook his questionable friendships with extremists and communists just so long as he kept his word and provided the "change" in America that he had promised.

Principles and Values: John McCain

McCain's values and principles have never been at question. His 5-year stint as a prisoner of war caused most Americans to admire and respect the man. He served his country well and even refused early release from his captors in exchange for a statement, which would have smeared the American military and government. He held fast to his beliefs under the most severe circumstances and this is an act for which he will always be respected.   In a speech at the Republican National Convention, McCain said, "I fell in love with my country when I was a prisoner in someone else's. I loved it not just for the many comforts of life here; I loved it for its decency, for its faith in the wisdom, justice and goodness of its people. I loved it because it was not just a place, but an idea, a cause worth fighting for. I was never the same again. I wasn't my own man anymore; I was my country's." Comments such as this have placed McCain high on the list of those that Americans revere.

McCain had continuously urged Americans to become more involved in government, saying that if you don't like how it's going, then join in and make a difference. This is the Spirit of America, a country long known for its willingness and ability to make a difference in the world; to contribute something worthwhile.

He has been accused by reporters and Washington insiders as being a man with a temper. When asked about this in a 2007 interview, he replied that he does get angry when he sees corruption in government, as well as pork barrel spending. He denied displaying any type of "temper tantrum" in public however, saying that his anger was attune to his fervor as a public servant and citizen concerned with justice and truth in govern-

ment and in the world around us. In a first and also an incident that can be classified as one of those events that can "only
happen in America", during the campaign Palin's daughter became pregnant out of wedlock. Palin's family stood by her and
respectfully asked the news to back off of exploiting the girl
and the family for political purposes. There was mixed opinion about whether this incident hurt the McCain campaign. It
was handled as well as could be expected and it showcased an
American family in turmoil, but working through the difficulties with integrity. The Palin family supported each other just
as American families should, so it's possible that this event may
have actually helped the McCain campaign. In spite of her lack
of experience, McCain fully and enthusiastically supported his
choice for vice-president, Sarah Palin. He was quick to make
the point that she governed the largest state in the USA, as well
as controlling 20% of America's oil. Even when the tides turned
and the media bashed Palin for her lack of experience, McCain
stood steadfastly by her side.

A People Desperate for Change!
Analyzing the Elements

As historians analyze the Presidential campaign of 2008,
they may find some Key Factors, which influenced the election results in Obama's favor. Of significance is the Influence of
Oprah Winfrey, her fans, and improved use of technology. This
new age of social networking and blogging had a profound effect upon public opinion and ultimately election results.

For the first time in history, the election outcome was mon-
itored by social networking sites, such as Facebook and Twit-
ter as it was by political organizers, consultants, and campaign
managers. Future politicians wishing to be elected will do well
to take note of this as well as advantage. The enormous benefit of utilizing such sites as these to sway voters and opinions
should not be underestimated in upcoming elections. Take this
into consideration: Barack Obama's MySpace page was able
to reach out to 160,000 people within a few weeks. In years
gone by, it might have taken 6 or more months for a campaign

to reach this number of voters. Obama's Facebook page garnered an incredible 200,000 supporters within a mere 2 weeks. A candidate has never before in history accomplished such a feat. Howard Dean's campaign manager, Joe Trippi, said this: "It took our campaign 6 months to get 139,000 people on an email list. It took one Facebook group barely a month to get to 200,000. That's astronomical."

At one college rally, Obama drew thousands of students. The rally was organized by college students who planned the entire event using Facebook. Obama never even met the college organizers until the day he arrived at the event.   And so the impact of technology and Internet-savvy voters has caused a huge ripple in the sea of political endeavor. Politics will never be the same again!

A second cause for the outcome of the election was the matter of a simple equation. This is one that has affected many campaigns over the years and one, which cannot be overcome: George Bush = Republican = low approval ratings and lack of confidence from American voters, McCain = Republican = No expectation of better governing and changes significant to turn the country around. The need for a change in the direction the nation was moving became paramount in the last days of George Bush's terms. But it is never more pronounced than in the following exchange between McCain and Obama during the third presidential debate in October of 2008: Obama: "When President Bush came into office, we had a budget surplus and the national debt was a little over $5 trillion. It has doubled over the last eight years." McCain: "Senator Obama, I am not President Bush. If you wanted to run against President Bush, you should have run four years ago. I'm going to give a new direction to this economy in this country."

Unfortunately for McCain, American voters, especially business men and women, were not willing to take the chance and believe that McCain might actually be able to move the nation in a new direction. There were too many factors against him. They chose instead, the complete opposite of McCain. They chose a Junior Senator from Illinois and America's first black president, a man whose views and politics stood in direct opposition to those of McCain and yes, of Bush.

Inevitable Conclusions

In the end, Obama somehow managed to tap into a need. There was a deep, undercurrent of dissatisfaction among the American people. They were sick of the way big government does business. They were tired of the lies handed down from Washington politicians for so many years. They'd had their fill of political rhetoric and speechifying. They were ready for the change that Barack Obama was promising. With the whole country in such dire financial straits that many were losing their savings and retirement monies, it seemed like change was long overdue. Also many Americans have come to love Oprah Winfrey for whom she is, a black woman with lots to give, someone who through her daily shows has encouraged them to cast aside their differences in search of common solutions. Ms Winfrey commands respect and enjoys admirations of millions of her fans, who take any suggestions of hers seriously; it appears that her suggestion to give Senator Barack Obama a chance to lead the US was taken to heart.

Most politicians will not spell out in black and white exactly what their views, intentions and beliefs are. In that regard, Obama is to be admired for his forthrightness. Normally, politicians approach their campaign by figuring out exactly what they believe the public wants to hear and then they pander to those needs, writing all their speeches with that information in mind.   But by doing this, they are keenly aware that many of the promises they've made to the public are not actually feasible and therefore will not be kept. For this reason, they do not want to have all those promises in one convenient document that can easily be viewed, read and understood. They scatter their promises out over the airwaves in many forms and on many venues, thus making it difficult to go back and see whether promises made were promises kept. By publishing his document, "Blueprint for Change", Obama doesn't leave himself much of an outlet for escape should he fail to keep all the campaign promises he has made to the American public. They are all there in black and white for anyone who wishes to read them.

After Obama's first year in office, there will certainly be those who will drag the document out into public light and make their pronouncements concerning Obama's ability to create the changes in American society and government that he espoused. In a country like America, this is inevitable. But it is also ironical that the very premise of his document relies on Americans coming together despite their differences and principles in an all-out joint effort to make our nation stronger and repair breaches in the society. Though many nations and people around the world admire and adore Americans, this is one of the elements that have set this nation apart from others. In times of crisis, we are able to lay aside our differences and work together to accomplish the task at hand. On a broader scale, the election of America's first African American president is a monumental feat that should not be diminished under any circumstances. Obama represents in every way, the "dream" that Martin Luther King Jr. believed was possible. He represents a new and healthier direction for America in the area of racial prejudice. Once a nation overcomes an issue as significant as racial prejudice, then the sky's the limit! Who knows what might be possible for the future of America. There is no telling what the US might achieve.

Prologue

Lessons of November 4th

Many news organizations had predicted an early night, due to what was described as a likely landslide win by Obama. Chicago was filled with supporters of Barack Obama; many who came did not mind the outcome. For a crowd that large, the atmosphere was filled with high expectations of real change, but more than just the spirit of hope there was the reality of a black man finally at the threshold of history, many wanted to be counted; a lot could hardly believe their chance at making history. Yet there were those who came with tears of joy and mixed blessings, hoping to savor the moment and just happy to witness the occasion.

As for me, the moment stood as triumph of *time*, it was time that allowed for change, it was time that created the moment of collapse of Wall Street, it was *time* that saw the dumb war in Iraq being fought on lies. It was time that witness how grown up men, chosen as leaders in a nation whose founding fathers, fought for equality, freedom and the pursuit of happiness, turned back every dial in the clock of liberty to satisfy their selfish greed and dimmed vision.

It has been said that it is with time that dark clouds are seen to fade and open the skies to a radiant sun. It is wisdom that men and women should strive to achieve better deal for themselves, it is only wise to know that wheel of change moves ever so slowly, but would come sooner that imagined, if only a few good people are willing to sacrifice their time for the good of all who have no voice, to offer a helping hand to those who need pulling up, to stand side by side with those who are suddenly becoming invincible, to hold the burning light for those who seek the way out of darkness.

I have learnt that it is time for those in Africa to stand up for their own future, and begin to build a better tomorrow for their children, it is time to eschew bitterness and embrace compassion, it is time to seek unity in the diversity of tongues, it is time for those who know to speak out. I have come to think that it is time that stolen and ill gotten wealth of African leaders, placed in civilized western world be returned for the good of Africans. It is time to truly free the slaves, from the shackles of their African slave masters, who in the name of governance seek to destroy the minds and land of their ancestors. Time might bring opportunity for change, but the change must be sought and brought on by the people. Progress towards change is a realization of common goals and limitations and deliberate efforts to achieve those goals, plus determination to surmount our challenges. Barack Obama is the 44th President of United States and the first black occupant of the white house.

It is time for change.

Appendix 1

Vice –President Joe Biden:

Joe Biden was born November, 20 1942 in Scranton, Pennsylvania to Joseph Robinette Biden Sr. and Catherine Eugenia;. He married his first wife Neilia Hunter in 1966; they had three children, Joseph "Beau" Biden (born 1969), Robert Hunter (born 1970) and Naomi Christina (1977). He lost his wife Neilia and his daughter Naomi Christina in an accident, a few weeks after he won the election as a US Senator. His two sons, who were also involved in the accident, and critically ill, later made full recovery.

He met Jill Jacobs, his present wife in 1995, through a blind date arranged by his brother, they became fond of each other and later got married in 1997. They have one daughter together, Ashley Blazer born in 1981.

Joe Biden attended University of Delaware and Syracuse University College of Law, where he received Jurist Doctor Degree in 1968.He started law practice in 1969 and within one year he ran for the office of the New Castle County Council under the Democratic Party platform. He ran for an elected office two years on in 1972 under the Democratic Party platform, seeking the office of US Senator from the state of Delaware. He won the election, thus becoming one of the youngest US Senators. A very devoted single father, Joe Biden rode the Amtrak trains for over one hour and half, back and forth capitol hill each day to be home for his two sons after the death of their mother.

Senator Joe Biden was re-elected six times as US Senator, becoming one of the longest serving Senators from Delaware. He served as US Senate Foreign Relations Chairman from 2001 through 2003 and again after the Democrats won the majority seats in the Senate, from 2007 till he resigned from the US Senate officially January 15th 2009. He also served as the Chairman of U.S. Senate Committee on the Judiciary, from 1987 until 1995.

Appendix 2

The Primaries Result- Democrats

State	Caucus	Won	Delegates
Iowa	Yes	Barack	27
Washington	Yes	Barack	53
Dc		Barack	11
Maine	Yes	Barack	15
Hawaii	Yes	Barack	14
Wisconsin		Barack	42
Vermont		Barack	9
Wyoming	Yes	Barack	7
Mississippi	Yes	Barack	20
South Carolina		Barack	33
Alabama		Barack	27
Alaska	Yes	Barack	10
Colorado	Yes	Barack	36

Connecticut	Yes	Barack	26
Delaware	Yes	Barack	9
Georgia		Barack	61
Idaho	Yes	Barack	15
Illinois		Barack	104
Kansas	Yes	Barack	23
Minnesota	Yes	Barack	48
Missouri		Barack	36
N Dakota	Yes	Barack	8
Utah		Barack	14
Louisiana	Yes	Barack	34
Nebraska	Yes	Barack	16
Texas	Yes	Barack	38
N Carolina		Barack	67
Oregon		Barack	31
Montana		Barack	9
Maryland		Barack	42
New Hampshire		Clinton	9
Michigan		Clinton	35
Nevada	Yes	Clinton	11
Massachusetts		Clinton	55
New Jersey		Clinton	59

New Mexico		Clinton	14
New York		Clinton	139
Oklahoma		Clinton	24
Tennessee		Clinton	40
Ohio		Clinton	75
Rhode Island		Clinton	13
Texas		Clinton	63
Pennsylvania		Clinton	85
Indiana		Clinton	38
Kentucky		Clinton	23
Puerto Rico		Clinton	38
S Dakota		Clinton	9
W Virginia		Clinton	23
Florida		Clinton	52
Arizona	Yes	Clinton	31
California		Clinton	203
Arkansas		Clinton	27

Appendix 3

States	Votes	Percentage won	Winner
California.	8,274,473	61	Barack Obama
Colorado	1,288,576	54	Barack Obama
Connecticut	997,772	61	Barack Obama
Delaware	255,459	62	Barack Obama
District of Columbia	245,800	93	Barack Obama
Florida	4,282,074	51	Barack Obama
Hawaii	325,871	72	Barack Obama
Illinois	3,419,673	62	Barack Obama
Indiana	1,374,039	50	Barack Obama
Iowa	828,940	54	Barack Obama

Maryland	1,629,467	62	Barack Obama
Maine	421,923	58	Barack Obama
Massachusetts	1,904,097	62	Barack Obama
Michigan	2,872,579	57	Barack Obama
Minnesota	1,573,354	54	Barack Obama
Nevada	533,736	55	Barack Obama
New Hampshire	384,826	54	Barack Obama
New Mexico	472,422	57	Barack Obama
New Jersey	2,215,422	57	Barack Obama
New York	4,804,701	63	Barack Obama
North Carolina	2,142,651	50	Barack Obama
Ohio	2,933,388	52	Barack Obama
Oregon	1,037,291	57	Barack Obama
Pennsylvania	3,276,363	55	Barack Obama
Rhode Island	296,571	63	Barack Obama
Vermont	219,262	68	Barack Obama

Virginia	1,959,532	53	Barack Obama
Washington	1,750,848	58	Barack Obama
Wisconsin	1,573,354	54	Barack Obama
Alabama	1,266,546,	61	McCain
Alaska	193,841	60	McCain
Arizona	1,230,111	54	McCain
Arkansas	638,017	59	McCain
Georgia	2,048,759	52	McCain
Kansas	699,655	57	McCain
Kentucky	1,048,462		McCain
Louisiana	1,148278	59	McCain
Mississippi	724,597	56	McCain
Missouri	1,445,814	50	McCain
Montana	243,882	50	McCain
Nebraska	452,979	57	McCain
North Dakota	168,601	53	McCain
Oklahoma	960,165	66	McCain
South Carolina	1,034,896	54	McCain
South Dakota	203,054	53	McCain
Tennessee	1,479,178	57	McCain
Texas	4,479,328	55	McCain

Utah	596,030	63	McCain
West Virginia	397,466	56	McCain
Wyoming	164,958	65	McCain
Idaho	403,012	61	McCain

1   See Appendix 1

2   See Appendix 2